Haunted Wyoming

HAUNTED WYOMING

LINDA MOFFITT

Schiffer Publishing Ltd
4880 Lower Valley Road, Atglen, Pennsylvania 19310

Binoculars Icon: File Search © Norebbo. ***Courtesy of www.bigstockphotos.com.***

Other Schiffer Books by the Author:
Haunts of the Southwest, 978-0-7643-3597-6, $19.99
Washington's Haunted Hotspots, 978-0-7643-3277-7, $14.99

Other Schiffer Books on Related Subjects:
America's Historic Haunts, 978-0-7643-3700-0, $29.99
Ghost Towns of the Rockies, 978-0-7643-3569-3, $16.99

Schiffer Books are available at special discounts for bulk purchases for sales promotions or premiums. Special editions, including personalized covers, corporate imprints, and excerpts can be created in large quantities for special needs. For more information contact the publisher:

Schiffer Publishing Ltd.
4880 Lower Valley Road
Atglen, PA 19310
Phone: (610) 593-1777; Fax: (610) 593-2002
E-mail: Info@schifferbooks.com

For the largest selection of fine reference books on this and related subjects, please visit our website at:

www.schifferbooks.com

We are always looking for people to write books on new and related subjects. If you have an idea for a book, please contact us at the above address.

This book may be purchased from the publisher.Include $5.00 for shipping. Please try your bookstore first. You may write for a free catalog.

In Europe, Schiffer books are distributed by
Bushwood Books
6 Marksbury Ave.
Kew Gardens
Surrey TW9 4JF England
Phone: 44 (0) 20 8392 8585; Fax: 44 (0) 20 8392 9876
E-mail: info@bushwoodbooks.co.uk
Website: www.bushwoodbooks.co.uk

Library of Congress Control Number: 2011930648

Designed by Stephanie Daugherty
Type set in Demon/NewBskvll BT

ISBN: 978-0-7643-3896-0
Printed in the United States of America

Dedication

For my family who supports me endlessly, regardless of my seemingly crazy ideas.

Acknowledgments

I wish to thank everyone who helped me put this book together and the many more who took the time to tell me their spirited stories and helped me find haunted locations across the state of Wyoming.

Contents

INTRODUCTION

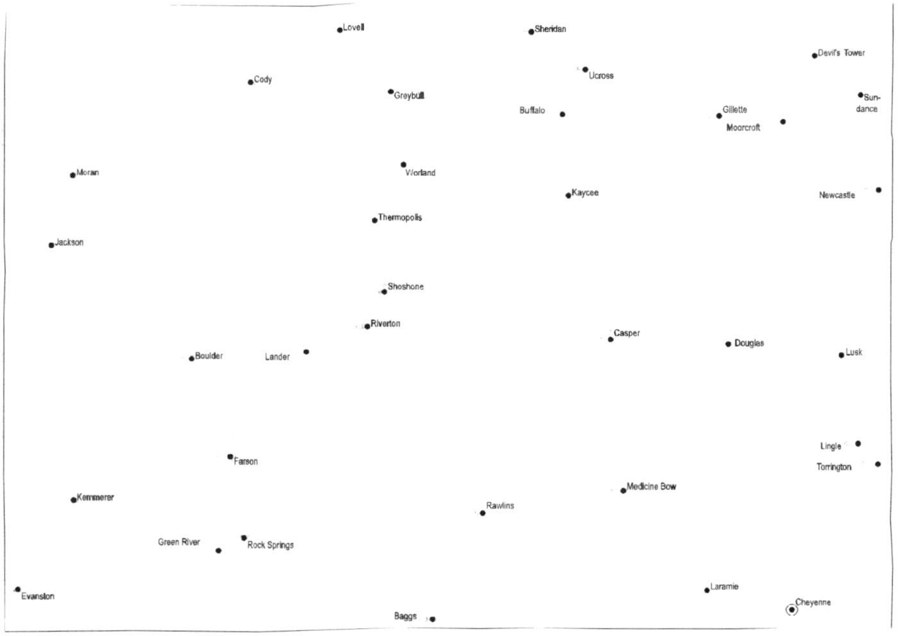

Wyoming is full of wonders. From Yellowstone National Park to Liberty Rock, there are many sites to see that astound tourists and residents alike. In 1807, John Colter wrote about his time spent in Yellowstone, though at the time many of his reports were considered fiction. The sights he found were so mysterious...even today Yellowstone is considered almost alien in its terrain.

Once a place where American Indians and buffalo roamed with freedom, white settlers soon came to this wondrous land. Hardship was an understatement, as winters were long and hard and the summers hot and unforgiving. Indian attacks were common and strange animals ruled the land. Long before white settlers came to Wyoming dinosaurs roamed the plains; and after, legends of mysterious creatures mingled with the American Indians. The American settlers were dreaming of the riches that hid beneath the earth and nothing would deter them from their fortunes. Later cowboys herded cattle across the empty state; now only a few highways cross the land.

The name "Wyoming" is said to derive from the Delaware Indian word "Maughwauwama," meaning "large plains." Wyoming is the tenth largest state and holds the smallest population. Its induction into the United States was July 10, 1890, when it became the forty-fourth state.

You can still find cowboys, Indians, and lots of lore. There are sacred sites and tourist traps. Sadly, however, some of the sacred sites *are* the tourist traps.

The American Indians remain a large part of Wyoming. They still keep their traditions alive on the land their ancestors roamed, and their culture is filled with legends and lore including ghost stories. The following tale is a ghost story from the Sioux Indians.

> Once lived a young maiden. She was very beautiful and sought after by all the men of the tribe, but she preferred the single life and each proposal was met with a firm "No" by the young maiden.
>
> One day the maiden fell ill and each day her sickness grew worse. Many different medicine men were called in to treat her, but to no avail. Two weeks later she succumbed to her illness. The whole camp mourned the loss of this maiden, especially her many suitors.
>
> She was taken several miles away and rolled in the finest robes and blankets and placed upon the scaffold that was built for her. After the maiden's funeral, her parents gave away all their horses, all their fine robes and blankets, and all of their daughter's belongings. Finally, they cut off their hair and dressed themselves in the poorest clothing they could find.
>
> A year came and went, but the parents refused to stop mourning for their daughter, claiming they had nothing further to live for now that their daughter had passed.
>
> The following year a hunter and his wife passed the scaffold that held the young maiden. Not far from the scaffold lay a stream bordered with sweet green grass. The hunter and his wife made camp near the stream for the night and erected a small teepee. Once it got dark the hunter's dogs started barking aggressively. The wife looked out the door and declared a woman was coming from the direction of the scaffold. Expecting it was the dead girl, the hunter told his wife not to be afraid and let the girl come. Soon there were footsteps near the door. The hunter called out to the visitor that they were welcome to come in and have something to eat.
>
> The figure came in slowly and sat near the door with its robes drawn tightly over its face. A plate of food was placed in front of the woman, but she did not move. They turned away from her and again offered for her to eat the food. Quickly the figure started eating the pieces of

deer meat on the plate. When finished the figure pushed the plate away and returned to sit silently.

The hunter asked the figure if it was the maiden who had passed a year ago and was placed on the scaffold. The figured nodded. Then he asked the maiden if she would sleep in the teepee with the couple; she shook her head no. Finally, the hunter asked if she would return the next night and the maiden nodded her head.

The maiden returned the following three nights and on the third night the hunter saw one of the maiden's hands. It was black and shriveled to the bone. The hunter rose up and rifled through a medicine sack he had hanging on a pole. Finding what he needed he started mixing and mashing some roots with skunk oil and vermillion.

He offered to rub some on the maiden assuring her the ointment would help with her complexion. The maiden agreed, and he began rubbing the maiden's blackened withered skin with the ointment. After, she rose up and returned to the scaffold.

The next day the hunter moved closer to the village and again his dogs started barking, alerting him that the maiden had found his new camp. The maiden entered the teepee, but this time she kept her robes loosely around her body and face. The hunter's wife offered the maiden a plate of food and the maiden did not hesitate reaching out for the plate, revealing fleshy hands. After the meal the hunter asked if the lotion helped with her skin, and the maiden nodded. The hunter made another batch and again applied it to the maiden. Afterwards the hunter asked if she would come with them to the village the next day; she shook her head no. His last question was if she was going to return to the village and see her parents. She shook her head with a "yes," rose up, and disappeared into the darkness.

The next day the hunter and his wife reached the village, and the hunter instructed his wife to invite the maiden's parents for dinner. The hunter and his wife then explained to the old couple that their daughter would join them for dinner and not to be afraid. Soon the dogs started barking and the young maiden entered the teepee. She was renewed with life... her skin natural and youthful looking. Her parents clung to her and begged her to return home with them, but she refused and stayed with the hunter and his wife who brought her back to life.

It was not long before she married the hunter, becoming his second wife. Soon he was called away for a war party. The two women waited and waited, but he did not return home. He was killed in battle.

The beautiful maiden waited a year before she married again; this husband was killed for stealing some horses. The third husband went off to war and, like the first one, was killed on the battlefield. Men started to fear her saying that she was holy. The maiden never again married and took up medicine. She lived many more years and as a very old lady she felt death approaching. When it was time, she asked her tribe members to take her where she had rested once before. The now frail woman crawled to the top of the new scaffold and wrapped herself in robes and blankets. Covering her face, she fell asleep once again... From this sleep there will be no more awakening.

Through research and interviews I have found that many of the ghosts in Wyoming are from around the same time. They usually came from the east in search of fortunes and found a home in Wyoming; many of the ghosts were rich and powerful men and women in their time and are remembered today through the large houses and even larger businesses they built. Some of the ghosts are well-known. Buffalo Bill Cody came to Wyoming and started building. He loved the state so much he built several hotels and has a town or two named after him.

The town of Cody is intertwined with Buffalo Bill, with Wild West shows still performed there. You may not get to see Sitting Bull, Annie Oakley, or even Buffalo Bill at the show, but if you stick around long enough you may just encounter one or all of their spirits still hanging around. Besides Cody and his famous friends, you may encounter the spirits of presidents and even a king or queen.

Yellowstone has been a very popular site to visit since it was discovered. The hazards that so many past residents and tourists faced are still there, but walkways and signs have been put up to deter you from falling in a boiling pool of water or breathing in toxic gas. Nearly a quarter of America's presidents have visited and stayed at one of the lodges located within its boundaries. President Roosevelt even shot a lion while visiting the park and President Carter ate pizza in the employee pub at the Lake Hotel, leaving his signature on the wall.

A Few Words of Caution

For all the sites listed, private or not, please follow all rules and signs posted. Wyoming is a sacred place for many. Do not litter or deface any of the monuments and buildings in any way. Do not light candles as they may start a fire, or draw on or in any of the sites. Finally, do not leave trinkets or take anything from these sites. If the sites are remote, tell someone where you are going, and always bring a map, water, and of course this book.

Never bother people, as some are not open to being interviewed. If you would like to visit a private residence, inquire, and make arrangements with the owner. Do not knock on their door or call repeatedly.

At the time of this writing the addresses and businesses featured were as stated, but some may have changed names and some of the spirits may have followed the owners to their new location or moved on. Some hauntings also occasionally fade away, or resurface, after renovation at a site has occurred. As for the directions provided, the same applies. Some roads and names may have changed since the publication of the book. Check before you leave to ensure the correct directions. I have tried my best to provide you with the best possible route through Wyoming, and please keep in mind that Yellowstone and other historic sites might be closed due to weather. So plan your trip there accordingly.

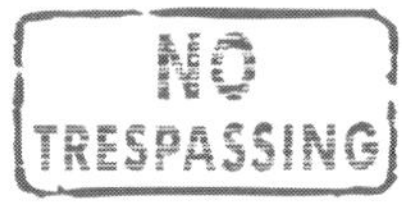

Understand that American Indians are protective of their sacred sites and land. Please do not take anything from the site or leave anything when you go. Remember karma does not care what race you are: It *will* come back to you.

I have tried to provide you with the best and most credible sources. I have spent countless hours interviewing witnesses, pouring over archives, reading newspaper articles, and exploring Wyoming. Some of the stories, of course, are legend, and still more are urban legends. I find these stories entertaining and have included some with the thought I would like to go there or hear that story, whether it be true or not. I like the choice to decide for myself and I hope you will as well.

This book is intended to help bring the history of Wyoming alive. It is meant to show you where to go, give you a bit of history behind the place, and tell you about the possible haunting. It is not meant to tell you everything behind the story, which is for you to find out and experience for yourself. Check into a hotel for the night and sleep with the ghosts. This book will tell you where and what to look for and which room to request. Although many of the locations listed have had paranormal investigations, for the most part I have not included findings from such reports. I want you to experience it for yourself. Have a picnic by Mattie's grave in Yellowstone National Park — do you feel her there with you...in the place she loved the most?

TRIP 1

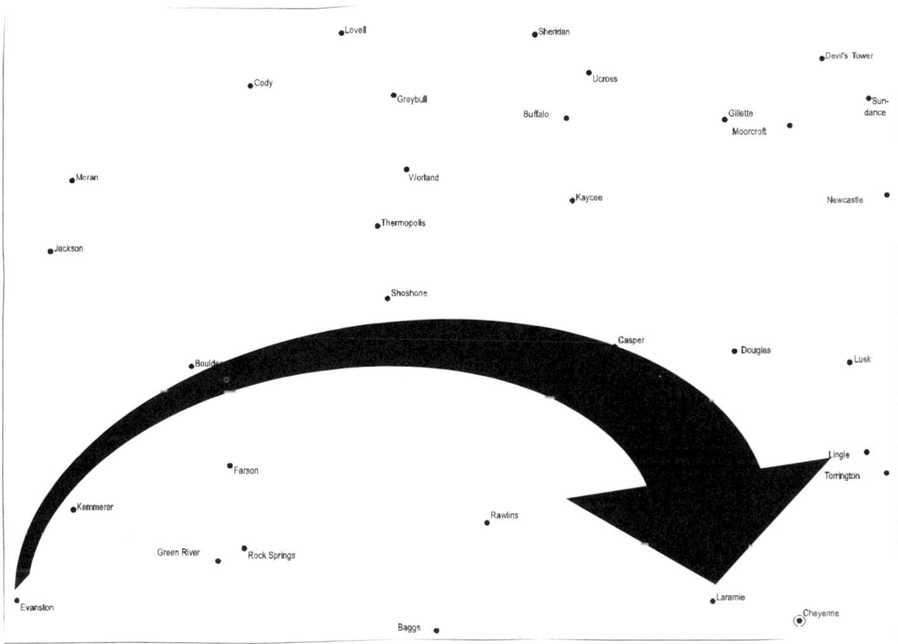

EVANSTON TO LARAMIE

EVANSTON

Like many towns in Wyoming, Evanston popped up overnight. It's named after a Union Pacific Railroad surveyor, James E. Evans. Before the train tracks even reached Evanston, the town had a Harvey House, followed by a roundhouse, and a machine shop.

Located along the First Transcontinental Railroad, the town was mainly populated with Chinese railroad workers. By the 1930s most of the Chinese population had moved on from the railroad town.

WYOMING STATE HOSPITAL

831 Highway 150 S,
Evanston, Wyoming 82930
www.health.wyo.gov/statehospital

The Wyoming State Hospital for the Insane opened its doors in 1887. There were many different reasons to be admitted to the hospital at that time. In 1897, the State Board of Charities noted that the year before, in 1896, twenty-three people were admitted for such reasons as intemperance, vicious habits, business worry, grief, and seduction.

The original building housed the male patients on the first floor and the female patients on the second floor. The basement of the building housed the kitchen, laundry, and storerooms. Today the facility is much different, with twenty-five buildings housing everything from a chapel to a country store.

Through the years reports have run rampant of paranormal happenings throughout the old hospital building. Residents and employees claim to see floating balls of light moving down the hallways and in the rooms. Unexplained sounds are heard in the building and rocking chairs occasionally sway back and forth, creaking, only to stop when someone comes near them to investigate.

One story that has haunted the hospital is about a sheet that covers a window facing the interstate. According to rumors, the sheet was hung to shield the view of a ghostly reenactment of a young mentally unstable girl hanging herself in the room. According to sources, she hangs herself nightly. Today the room is used for storage.

Directions From Wyoming State Hospital to Fort Bridger: Head northwest on WY-150N and merge into I-80E towards Rock Springs. Take Exit 34 toward Fort Bridger and follow the signs.

Fort Bridger

Established in 1842 as a trading post, Fort Bridger was later a vital supply stop on the Oregon Trail. Later serving as a Military Post during the Utah War, the fort could not sustain itself and was closed in 1890. The town of Fort Bridger still lives on, incorporating parts of the historic fort in its town.

Fort Bridger State Park

(307) 782-3842
www.wyoparks.state.wy.us

There was once a ghost at the cemetery at Fort Bridger that liked to follow and help the caretaker out. He first appeared in June 1987, wearing a white cowboy hat. The caretaker eventually recognized him —it was the ghost of a man who had recently passed away. The man's wife still lived in the area. The following year, in May, the man's wife passed away and his spirit has not been seen since. Perhaps they were reunited in the afterlife.

Fort Bridger was established in 1842 as a fur outpost and supply stop along the Oregon Trail. Later the United States Army established a military post at the site; it was not long after the Utah War that the fort was shut down, but today a town named after the fort lives on. Some of the original fort buildings were incorporated into the town, including the Commanding Officer's Quarters, which was made into a hotel, and the stone barracks, which was turned into a milking barn. A few of the buildings are still standing and are open to the public including the 1888 Stone Barracks.

The cemetery is not the only place residents and visitors see spirits. Soldiers have been reported to walk down roads in formation. Lights have been seen dancing around the old fort's grounds and disembodied

Is this one of the men who hangs around Fort Bridger long after death? *Courtesy of the Library of Congress.*

voices are heard throughout the buildings. A phantom dog has even been seen wandering the fort's grounds.

Directions To Mi Casita Restaurant in Green River: From Fort Bridger, return to I-80E, exit at US-30/Rock Springs, and continue straight onto West Flaming Gorge Way.

Green River

Famous for being the first city in the United States to ban door-to-door salesmen, Green River had a rocky start. Incorporated in 1968, the town had nearly 2,000 residents, but when the railroad moved its division point to another spot many of the residents moved out as well, leaving a meek 101 residents in Green River. Luckily for a drought the railroad was forced to move the division point back to Green River, bringing most of its residents as well.

Mi Casita Restaurant

36 East Flaming Gorge Way
Green River, Wyoming 82935

While only one customer has seen the apparition of the woman who haunts this building, through the years many have claimed that this mischievous spirit makes her presence known in other ways.

In 2004, the space was home to Sage Creek Bagels; the owner, customers, and employees all had eerie experiences. The owner recounts, "We put a couple pounds of butter out to soften so that we could make cookies. When we came back, it had all been pushed off the counter and onto the floor." Once a pitcher full of water fell off the counter as a customer walked by. On another occasion a child who was in the basement had her hair pulled. The bells on the door would ring unexpectedly — with no one in sight — and the faucets were known to turn on by themselves.

The owner prior to Sage Creek Bagels also reported unexplained occurrences, but it is not known if the woman who haunts the building is happier now that it is a Mexican restaurant or still likes to play pranks on the current tenants and patrons.

Directions To Sweetwater County Historical Museum: From Mi Casita Restaurant, head northwest on West Flaming Gorge Way toward North Center Street.

Sweetwater County Historical Museum

3 East Flaming Gorge Way
Green River, Wyoming 82935
(307) 872-6435
www.sweetwatermuseum.org

It should be no surprise that many museums are haunted with all the artifacts they hold; after all, the dearly departed may not be able to so easily give up possession of these items. Spirits hang around all kinds of places: new buildings, historic buildings, and some are even content to follow their beloved item into private hands.

The Sweetwater County Historical Museum is one such place. In 2000, the museum moved to its current home — a 1931 Post Office. Prior to this move, it lived in the basement of the courthouse. The new courthouse was built on land that a previous courthouse sat on from 1871.

A prior curator of the museum claimed to have seen a man in the stacks who resembled a notable Green River resident. Mr. Hutton migrated to the United States with his family in 1887 and made his way to Green River in 1896. Hutton worked in the Union Pacific Railroad Hotel, as well as the town's first electric power plant. He later married and homesteaded in an area known as Hutton Heights. As a proud citizen of Green River, he went on to create the Community Club, which is now the Chamber of Commerce, and served as a volunteer fireman. Hutton also loved antiques and other curiosities. He was such an avid collector that a local newspaper reported hundreds of people came each year to visit his collections. After Mr. Hutton's death in 1974, the Sweetwater County Historical Museum acquired some of his collection.

Mr. Hutton loved his antiques and may have stuck around to ensure their safe-keeping or perhaps he was just checking up on the Green River residents. Either way, once the museum moved to its new location, Mr. Hutton has no longer been seen. He may still come from time-to-time to check on his antiques or perhaps he was attached to the courthouse.

The Post Office building may not have Mr. Hutton walking the corridors, but there is no lack of spirits keeping several of the staff spooked. Children playing loudly, shouting, and crashing objects have all been reported within the walls of the Post Office building. When staff investigate, nothing has been moved and no one is there.

Directions to Sweetwater County Library: From the Sweetwater County Historical Museum, head northwest on East Flaming Gorge Way toward Center Street. Take the first right onto East 2nd N Street and then the first left onto North 1st East Street.

Sweetwater County Library

300 North 1st East Street
Green River, Wyoming 82935
307-875-3615
www.sweetwaterlibraries.com

Established in 1892 the city's cemetery held an unknown number of deceased loved ones. As with many towns across the country, the city decided for various reasons to move the cemetery; hence, bodies were dug up and moved to another location. The Sweetwater Cemetery moved just up the hill to the Riverview Cemetery in 1926. Many old-timers remember stopping by and watching the decayed caskets being raised and bodies, occasionally, tumbling out as the wood caskets had started to crumble. Children would steal rings and other items from the deceased... even bones were occasionally taken by passersby.

The land that was cleared was used as a park until 1944, when building started on the site to erect housing to accommodate the large amount of veterans returning home from the war. During the construction of the housing site, bodies were found that had never been moved to the new cemetery. These poor souls were unknown and moved to Riverview Cemetery.

As the years passed, the Veteran's housing was slated to be torn down and rebuilt as a public library. During the construction, twelve more unknown bodies were discovered in 1978, with even more bodies dug up in 1983 while the grounds were being landscaped. The 1983 findings stirred up the community with the threat these bodies might have carried small pox. After some checking, these fears were quickly put to rest and the town went back to normal...sort of.

When these bodies were found, some of them were partially under the sidewalk or under the foundation of the building. Only part of the body could be moved leaving the rest buried where they lay. Grown men, women, and babies were found; some of them were still decomposing, hair was still intact on faces and heads, and some still had partial flesh on them. In 1985, the building started to sink and, during the structural work, another body was found — a small child. Encased in its coffin, the child's flesh was still preserved but badly decayed.

Employees of the library take all these findings in stride and try to keep a sense of humor about it. There are too many spirits that inhabit the library to tell you all the stories, as almost every worker has had some sort of experience. Patrons of the library have had experiences as well, so many in fact the library has created a website called the "Ghost Log Blog." They offer ghost tours and several paranormal television shows have come to the library to investigate.

Employees and patrons of the library have had doors open and close, toilets flushed by unseen hands, lights turned on and off, and objects moving about seemingly on their own accord. Ghostly conversations are heard as well and names have been called out. Many employees have seen apparitions in the library, walking among the stacks or just taking in the library's activities. One employee heard a piano playing one night, another saw balls of light bounce around, and still others say they have been touched. Since so many employees have been spooked, the library implemented a rule where no one could be in the building alone at night...just for the safety of the living. The spirits that remain seem to coexist nicely, but employees were afraid if they got startled and fell, they would lay there all night until staff came in to open up the next morning.

The spirits that remain under the library and surrounding area have been disturbed; some lost body parts in the move while others lost their identity. Is it any wonder then that they roam the library looking for a place to rest or, perhaps, for their story to be told?

Directions To Rock Springs City Hall: From Sweetwater County Library, head southwest on North 1st East Street toward East 3rd North. Take the Third left onto East Flaming Gorge Way and then the ramp to I-80e. Keep right and follow the signs to Rock Springs; exit at Dewar Drive and turn right onto Dewar Drive/ Us 30 Bus E. Turn right at Grant Street, right at A Street, left onto Broadway Street and then the third right onto D Street. City Hall is on the left.

Rock Springs

Hundreds of men were beaten and burned during the Rock Springs Massacre.
Courtesy of Library of Congress.

On September 2, 1885, just after seven in the morning, a group of white men ran into Coal Pit Number 6 yelling that the Chinese should not be permitted to work there. The Chinese in the mine tried to reason with the white men, but were quickly beaten; three of the Chinese workers lay injured by the time the foreman broke up the fight and stopped all work in the mine.

Upon pouring out of the mine all the white men in the area started to congregate, gathering weapons and firearms. The men marched into town and before long were assembled into a meeting hall. Around 2 p.m., they split into two mobs and made their way to "Chinatown." Surrounding it, they started firing their weapons. The first man shot was Lor Sun Kit. Even with the first death, the Chinese did not flee, standing their ground, until the white miners killed three more men.

One mob pressed into "Chinatown" while the other mob stood at the other end of town cutting off any sort of escape. When a Chinese man was met by a member of the mob, they were asked if they had a weapon. They then were either hit with the butt of a gun and robbed of his gold, silver, and other valuables, or just robbed and let go without a beating. Onlookers would shout and clap egging the white miners on. The houses in Chinatown were ransacked and robbed, not just by the men who worked in the mines, but by women and children as well.

After the robbing ceased, the houses were burned to the ground. Many of the Chinese who had been shot were thrown into the engulfed houses; in all, seventy-nine houses were burned down and, by 9 p.m., nothing remained of "Chinatown." The total number of Chinese killed was twenty-eight, with an additional fifteen people wounded.

The Chinese who wanted to return to "Chinatown" to either take care of the wounded or bury their dead could not, as there was no shelter left and no supplies. Instead they hid in the hills and, following the railroad tracks, made their way into Green River. The railroad telegraphed all engineers in the area to pick up any Chinese they found wandering along the tracks and bring them into Evanston.

When all the survivors finally gathered in Evanston on September 5th, they were met with more fury and threatened with the same horrible violence they had just escaped from. The United States Army stepped in and peace was restored. By September 9th, the troops were ordered to take the Chinese back to Rock Springs.

The Rock Springs Independent reported:

> "The return! Three hundred soldiers protecting them. Chinatown to be rebuilt. United and determined action needed. It was rumored Wednesday noon that the Chinese were on their way back to Rock Springs. Few believed the rumor, as it was not thought they could be induced to return. But about two o'clock a passenger train came in bearing two hundred armed soldiers. Closely following was a freight train of twenty-two cars loaded with 650 of the hated Chinese, the latter train switching off and went toward No. 3 mine, where the Chinese disembarked, and hurried over to the ruins of their houses. They began digging in the cellars and soon unearthed a large amount of money. Six thousand dollars in gold and silver was dug up from one cellar, and as much more from another, where it had been concealed before their flight. Numbers of them soon came up town. Some looked bold and defiant while others were evidently fearful of being attacked, but no demonstration was made against them. The cars were afterwards brought down the track to a point near the soldiers' camp, where the Chinamen built fires, had supper, and spent the night. The action of the company in bringing back the Chinese means that they are to be set to work in the mines, and that American soldiers are to prevent them

> from again being driven out. It means that all the white miners in Rock Springs, except those absolutely required, are to be replaced by Chinese labor. It means that the company intend to make a "Chinatown" out of Rock Springs, as they proposed to the Almy miners last Monday. It means that Rock Springs is killed, as far as white men are concerned, if such program is carried out."

Upon returning, "Chinatown" was a grim sight: badly burnt bodies, decomposing and partially eaten by pigs and dogs, lay in the streets and in the remains of buildings. The Chinese were overcome with grief and most wanted to leave. The troops provided clothes, provisions, and wagons to sleep in, as well as protection.

Names were taken and around fifty of the most violent men, including two women, were accused. On September 7th, twenty-two men were arrested and taken to the Green River jail. Among those arrested, according to *The New York Times,* was "Isaiah Whitehouse, member-elect of the Legislature." Furthermore, the newspaper reported: "There is no report of further trouble since the troops went to the scene of the disturbance. None is likely to occur in the presence of the troops."

Chinese and whites were paid by the amount of coal they brought up. When production needed to be increased, the white miners who were part of a union demanded higher wages. As a result, more Chinese were hired to work, since they were cheaper and not unionized. Tensions were already high between the two races in Rock Springs and after a meeting the white miners decided to take charge of the situation and run the Chinese out of town for good.

Nearly ten years later, in 1895, a City Hall building was built. The town, now incorporated, was not all Chinese as the white miners had feared, but a mix of both — and the town was booming. Today, ghost stories float around the town, but with all the tension leading up to and after the famous Rock Springs Massacre is it any wonder that a few spirits still remain?

City Hall

212 D Street
Rock Springs, Wyoming 82901
(307) 352-1538

The City Hall building is one such place plagued with ghost stories. Full-bodied apparitions are seen floating down the hallways and through the rooms of this historic building. Locked doors tend to unlock and open by themselves. One security guard claimed to have been thrown from his chair by an unseen force. Lights are seen floating in the building at night through the windows. Security guards could be the source of the balls of light, holding a flashlight as they walk down the hall. However, when the lights are seen, usually only one security guard is in the building, so how could multiple lights be seen on different floors?

Directions to The Saints Cyril and Methodist Parish Center: From City Hall, head northwest on D Street toward Broadway Street. Take the first right onto Broadway Street; continue onto M Street, and turn left at Pilot Butte Avenue.

The Saints Cyril and Methodist Parish Center

633 Bridger Avenue
Rock Springs, Wyoming 82901
(307) 382-9114

The Saints Cyril and Methodist Parish Center was once the location of the barracks set up to house the Army while they stayed in town to keep peace after the Chinese massacre. After the Army left, the barracks were turned into housing and quickly bought up. One family moved into their new home in the 1940s and could never have expected what they would take away from living in the house.

Shortly after the family moved in, sounds of running and playing in the house started up. One of the children recounted her nightly ritual, "I can remember my dad... he used to get up almost every single night and yell at myself and my three sisters and my brother for getting up and walking around the house. And we'd say 'Dad, we're not walking around the house, we're in bed.' And he'd say 'I can hear you, I can hear you clomping around.' And this went on for a long, long time; I don't remember how long. He finally was convinced that it wasn't us walking around because he'd get up every night and check everything and check everyone and make sure we were asleep. And finally, I don't know when, it dawned on us that we had things going on."

The spirits were known to open cupboards, turn on and off lights, open and close doors, and flush the toilets at all hours of the day and night. This lasted for years. Finally the family moved into a new home across the railroad tracks. Thinking this was the end of their ghostly inhabitants, they were relieved for the move...that is, until activity started up at their new house with increasing frequency. It turns out the spirits were attached to the family and followed them to their new home. The move upset them and they were now acting out more than ever showing their disapproval.

The spirits never showed themselves until the family moved. An intern at Rock Springs Historical Society wrote about the experience recounted from the family's daughter.

> "One night, when the father was alone in the house, he thought he heard something in the hall. When he looked out his bedroom door, he saw an elderly Chinese couple, two parents, and two or three children walk in the front door, down the hallway past him, and out to the back door. Since then, others in the family have also seen the ghosts. Two of the daughters, while taking care of their ill mother, reported seeing an apparition of a woman wearing a dress, and what they described as a porcelain mask of their mother's face."

The family has since moved on from this house, and the new owner reports nothing unusual. It is unknown if the spirits continued to follow the family or returned to the original building they inhabited while alive. The Chinese family is also unknown: did they perish during the Rock Springs Massacre and find solace in the Army Barracks?

Author's Note: Some say the Chinese buried their dead where the town has now built up, so perhaps the Chinese who died in the massacre are still walking the streets of Rock Springs looking for their families long after death. It is not known how many spirits still remain, some even reliving that horrible event so many years ago.

Directions to Carbon County Museum: From Saints Cyril and Methodist Parish Center, head east on Bridger Avenue, toward Pilot Butte Avenue, and turn right at 9th Street. Take ramp to I-80E and then take Exit 211 for WY-789N. Turn left at WY-789, left at 9th Street, and left at West Walnut Street.

Rawlins

While on-duty guarding the transcontinental railroad, General John A. Rawlins needed a drink of water. Immediately a scout party was on the hunt for a water source. They happened upon a spring. General Rawlins declared the water the best he had ever tasted and a town sprang up around the spring.

Carbon County Museum

904 West Walnut Street
Rawlins, Wyoming 82301
(307) 382-2740
www.carboncountymuseum.org

After removing the spikes from the Union Pacific Railroad's main line, George and his partners, who included Jessie James, his brother Frank, and Dutch Charley, hunkered down and waited for the train to derail for an easy robbery. Unfortunately, as they were pulling the spikes, a Union Pacific foreman in a handcar came around the bend and noticed something was out of place. He rode ahead and informed the train to stop and called lawmen to investigate. George and his partners shot two of the lawmen. Immediately, Jessie and Frank took off out of Wyoming. George and Dutch were not as smart. They got away, but not far. Dutch was caught in Montana and confessed; infuriated, the locals strung him up on a telegraph pole.

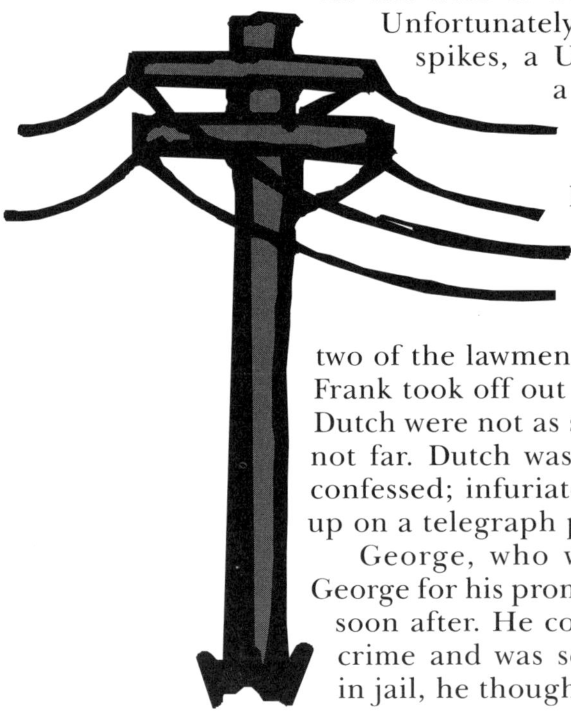

George, who was known as Big Nose George for his prominent feature, was caught soon after. He confessed right away to his crime and was sentenced to hang. While in jail, he thought it would be a good idea to get out of town and, filing off his leg irons, he knocked out the jailer. The citizens of Rawlins, though, had formed a lynching party and decided to go get George. Since he had knocked out his only security, George was easy prey for the increasingly drunk mob. They strung him up to a telegraph pole in front of Fred Wolfe's Saloon and told him to jump off the box he was standing on. George refused, so a member of the mob kicked the box out from under his feet. Fortunately for George the rope parted. Unfortunately the mob had another rope handy. They put a ladder against the pole, forced George up it again, and then pulled the ladder away from him. George hung onto the pole for dear life. Eventually he grew tired and gained himself a painful and slow death, especially since the noose rubbed off his ears.

If that weren't enough... After being placed in his coffin, it would not shut — apparently Big Nose George's nose was even too big for his coffin. Excessive pressure had to be applied to shut the lid before the nails were driven into it.

Dr. Osborne in his younger years. *Courtesy of Library of Congress.*

Two local doctors Thomas Maghee and John Osborne thought it would be great to examine the cadaver of an outlaw. Maghee wanted the brain and Osborne...well, he wanted revenge. According to legend, Osborne was on the train that George and his friends tried to derail and rob. Dr. Osborne skinned George, taking his thigh skin and chest skin. He made a doctor's bag, coin purse, and a pair of shoes with the dead man's flesh. After the pair of doctors had their way with poor ol' George, they hid his remains in a whiskey barrel and buried him. In the 1950s,

Are these the shoes made from Big Nose George's skin? *Courtesy of Library of Congress.*

while doing construction, a whiskey barrel was dug up with what remained of George's bones inside.

Dr. Maghee gave the skull cap to a medical student. Dr. Lillian Nelson later became the first female doctor in Wyoming, and used the skull piece as an ashtray and, on some accounts, a doorstop.

Now the story really gets weird. Dr. Osborne loved wearing his new shoes. He later became a bank chairman, the largest sheep owner in the territory, and the governor of Wyoming. Governor Osborne wore his Big Nose George shoes to his inauguration.

While you are checking out Osborne's shoes at the Carbon County Museum, make sure to also look at George's death mask — it's earless.

The Dean/Summer House

Author's note: The Dean/Summer House is a private residence; continue on for directions to the Ferris Mansion

On Spruce Street sits a quiet duplex — or so the families of Lois Dean and Diantha Summer thought. In the 1970s, this duplex was turned upside down with terrifying attacks and paranormal occurrences.

At first, just scratching sounds came from outside the house and then the lights started malfunctioning. The two families thought it was the wiring and had the whole house rewired, but the problem continued and soon they began feeling an ominous presence in the house and near the garage. Fourteen-year-old Mike Summer was out back by the garage when he was suddenly tossed into the air and thrown some five feet to the ground by a mysterious force.

One quiet afternoon Lois and Diantha were working in the garage when they noticed a female shaped dark mist hovering in one of the corners. Approaching it, Diantha described the dark shape as "something black and cold started coming out of it...like strands of ribbons." The ribbons of darkness wrapped themselves around Diantha. Paralyzed with fear Dianatha stood frozen until Lois lunged toward Diantha and broke the spell.

The Garage Witch has continued to frighten the inhabitants of the duplex despite the house being blessed. The occurrences have seemed to slow down and lessen, but the Garage Witch always remains.

In the early 1900s, a small church graveyard was located on the property. When the bodies were exhumed and moved to the Rawlins Cemetery, two bodies were left unaccounted for. The two graves are thought to be under the garage....

Directions to Ferris Mansion Bed and Breakfast: From Carbon County Museum, head east on West Walnut Street toward 9th Street; take the second right onto 8th Street and then make the first left onto West Maple Street.

Ferris Mansion Bed and Breakfast

607 West Maple
Rawlins Wyoming 82301
(307) 701-3961
www.ferrismansion.com

George Ferris never saw the completion of his Queen Anne home overlooking Rawlins. He broke ground on his fabulous mansion in 1899, and was planning on showing his ascension into the state's elite with this showpiece. Ferris was one of Wyoming's prominent businessmen and a member of the House and Territorial Legislative Assemblies. Ferris also owned the Ferris-Haggarty copper mine. Sadly, Ferris was killed when he was thrown from a carriage near his mine, leaving his widow Julia to finish the construction of his home.

It seemed the house was doomed to be haunted from the start. While working on the roof, a worker fell three stories to his death and then, just after the mansion's completion, Julia grieved again when her youngest son, Cecil, was shot by his older brother while playing with a loaded gun. Julia lost four out of seven of her children to strange accidents.

The house has had many occupants over the years; at one time the house was even turned into apartments. Currently the house has undergone renovations and is beautifully restored and is now open as a bed and breakfast.

Visitors and occupants of the house claim to have seen two boys playing in what was the playroom; one possibly is Cecil, Ferris's youngest son. A woman in Victorian dress has been seen outside watering flowers that are no longer there. Is this Julia still tending to her home? It seems that from the first death in the house poltergeist activity has been reported while strange sounds and knocking has been heard. Televisions and other electrical devices turn on and off by themselves. The kitchen is where Julia, dressed in a long nightgown, and Cecil are most seen, sometimes together.

Directions to Frontier Prison: From Ferris Mansion Bed and Breakfast, head east on West Maple Street towards 6th Street and take the first left onto 6th Street. Turn right at West Walnut Street.

Frontier Prison

500 West Walnut Street
Rawlins, Wyoming 82301
(307) 324- 4422
www.wyomingfrontierprison.org

Built in the early 1900s, the Frontier Prison was supposed to relieve pressure on the overcrowded Territorial Prison. However, the 'Old Pen,' as it is more commonly known, was just as crowded. All the inmates were moved from the Territorial Prison into their new home, which consisted of 104 cells. There was no electricity or running water and soon all the cells were just as cramped as the Territorial Prison. Several additions were completed to the prison by 1904, but it seemed the prison could not escape the influx of criminals sentenced to its walls.

Security at the prison was lax; in 1912, over a two-day span, thirty prisoners escaped through the barbed wire and the wooden stockade. In 1915, the concrete walls and towers that surround the prison today were finished, which helped to deter escape attempts. The following year the 'Death House' was completed. The Death House housed death row inmates, the gallows, and later the gas chamber.

The prison closed in 1981 and then sat vacant for several years. In 1987, a low-budget movie starring a young Viggo Mortensen was filmed there; unfortunately, significant damage was done to the prison, as it was not yet considered an historic site. The Frontier Prison is currently an historical site; a museum operates out of there and is open for outside events, including tours...especially at Halloween.

Life was hard at the prison. If prisoners broke the rules, they were handcuffed to the 'punishment pole' and whipped with leather straps and later rubber hoses. The rowdier ones were sent to solitary confinement, naked, for up to six weeks.

Fourteen men took their last breath at the prison. Nine men were hanged with the prison's Julien Gallows, a unique way of hanging in which the prisoner's weight tripped a switch that allowed water to fill a bucket and ultimately release the trap door the condemned person was standing on. Tom Horn was one of the first to meet his fate by this device in 1903. The other five men were executed via gas chamber, which replaced the Julien Gallows in 1937.

Ghosts are so common at the prison you can barely escape visiting the site without hearing an unearthly knock or experiencing something more. Andrew Pixley was an extremely violent man. Murdering and cannibalizing two young girls, he was sentenced to death for his crimes. Though executed in the 1960s, he continues his angry and violent ways within the prison's walls.

Pixley is not the only spirit that remains in the prison. Visitors and guides report feeling an oppressed pressure on their chests near the shower and the death house. Screams from ungodly spirits bellow from the gallows room and gas chambers. Knocking and footsteps are heard in broad daylight all around the prison, as well as voices and other daytime prison activities. Ghostly figures have even been seen as reflections in glass and around corners darting off into the distance.

Be prepared if you take a tour... A long-deceased prisoner might be escorting you on your journey into the past. If you are looking to see what it would feel like to be incarcerated at the prison, check out the prison's website. They offer all-night lock downs where you are actually locked in a cell — very possibly with its ghostly inhabitant.

Directions To Rawlins High School and Middle School: From Frontier Prison, head east on West Walnut Street toward 4th Street and take the first left onto 3rd Street. Turn right at Colorado Street and then take the first left onto East Brooks Street. Turn left at Harshman Street.

Rawlins High and Middle School

Rawlins Middle School
1500 Harshman Street
Rawlins, Wyoming 82301
(307) 328-9205

Three acres make up the area where the Rawlins High School and Middle School are located, and they share a common denominator with the residential houses surrounding them — they all have reported ghostly apparitions of Indians and Pioneers roaming their yards and hallways. The whole area that surrounds the schools is an Indian Burial Ground and an old pioneer trail. A few blocks away from the middle school may be the portal to the Indian spirit world. Two houses are reported to have a heap of activity, far more than their neighbors. Full-bodied apparitions appear, objects move, locked doors open by themselves, chairs rock, and disembodied voices have been heard and caught on a tape recorder.

Now that you know a bit about the surrounding area, I will dive into the haunting of the high school. Rumors speculate about why the high school is haunted; some say that while the high school was being built a worker fell to his death from a catwalk in the auditorium. The auditorium is where most of the ghostly sightings occur. 'Siberia,' the area under the stage where the sets and props are kept, is known as a hot spot of activity. Many strange noises come from this area, including the sound of props moving and crashing. Upon investigation nothing has been moved or broken. Lights turn on and off by themselves and objects move around the spacious building, with some even disappearing only to be found later. One employee of the school claimed to hear voices and conversations in the auditorium when he was the only one present.

The Middle School is full of spirits that like to interact with the living. Besides objects moving and electrical disturbances, apparitions have been seen all over the building. One janitor had an especially eerie experience as she cleaned up one classroom. A short, well-dressed man appeared out of the darkened room and approached the janitor; she asked him for his name and what he wanted. The man quickly ran out of the room and down the hallway. The janitor took chase, but, upon turning the corner, noticed he no longer had a head! He then faded away. Who was this man and what did he want from the janitor? After telling her story the next day a few of the other janitors confessed that they too had similar experiences at the school and one janitor even quit rather than work nights at the school. A woman in white has been seen floating near the windows of the science room; she has also been seen in the music room and the boy's locker room. A policeman called to the school one evening spotted the intruder. As he shined his flashlight on the woman standing in the corner, she faded away before his very eyes.

Directions To Wyoming Territorial Prison: From Rawlins Middle School, head south on Harshman Street towards East Brooks Street. Turn left at US-287S and take the ramp to I-80E. Take Exit 311 and turn left at WY-130/ Snowy Ridge Road. Take the second left onto West Garfield Street and then turn right.

SIGHTINGS

The Ghost of Slaughterhouse Gulch

In 1918, two couples were camped out between Encampment and Battle, sitting close to the newly built fire to keep warm, when surprisingly a cough rang out through the night. The four campers looked up to see a miner walking along the road. He did not look toward the people or even acknowledge their presence. This was odd since no one was around and it was dark out. Where was the man going? Why did he not come to the fire to warm himself? The strange man continued walking along the road until he was finally out of sight. This man puzzled the campers; he had no horse or supplies and even more strange was that when he passed the campers no one heard his footsteps.

This was not the first encounter with the ghost of Slaughterhouse Gulch. On another occasion a stagecoach driver claimed a man approached his team of six horses. As he walked right between the horses,

A spirit walked right through a team of horses attached to a stagecoach that looked just like this one. *Courtesy of Library of Congress.*

the man disappeared. The horses were spooked and reared up. If this were a living man, the horses would have killed him. Stranger yet was when he disappeared into thin air. The stagecoach driver resigned after recounting this story to his boss.

According to legend, the ghost that roams the Slaughterhouse Gulch area is an unfortunate miner who, in a mining explosion, was blown literally to pieces. He could not be laid to rest properly since not all the pieces of his body could be found. Is the ghost of Slaughterhouse Gulch looking for his body? No one knows for sure why he still roams the countryside, but when you go camping, keep your eyes and ears out for a miner who may or may not approach you.

SIGHTINGS

Nimerigar

In every culture there are tales of giants, dragons, fairies, leprechauns, and an assorted mix of other creatures that have disappeared over time or only live in far off places. Wyoming is not so far-off. Ancient American Indian tribes — the Arapaho, Sioux, Cheyenne, and Crow — still carry on their traditions and customs here, and one legend that comes from them is that of little people.

The Shoshone Indians of Wyoming often tell a tale of the Nimerigar. After some research, I learned that the name "Nimerigar" is not a Shoshone word since Shoshone words end with vowels, not consonants. Perhaps the name is borrowed from another tribe or has been changed over the years for the white man. Nonetheless, the Nimerigar are a fierce race of little people with canine teeth who attack the Shoshone with tiny bows and poisoned arrows. When the Nimerigar became too ill and was a burden to their community, another Nimerigar would kill the sick with a blow to the head.

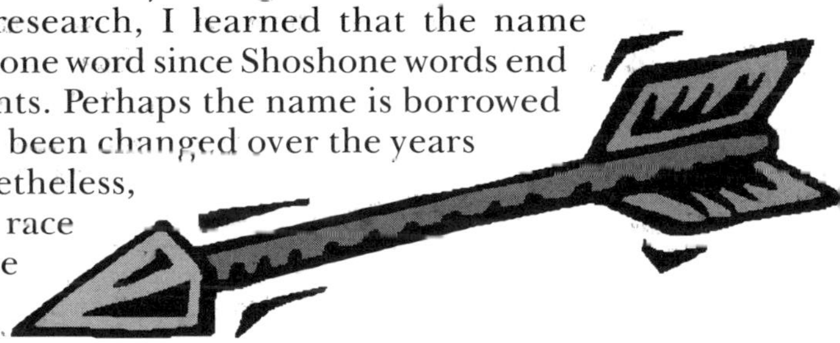

These tales passed from the Indians to the white man, with the white man always chuckling about how silly the Indians were. They never put much stock into the stories...until in 1932 two miners found a tiny skeleton.

Cecil Main and Frank Carr were two prospectors looking for gold in Pedro Mountain. Blasting a rock wall revealed a cave where a fourteen-inch tall little mummy was sitting on a ledge, cross-legged, with its hands resting in its lap. The creature was so well preserved in its little home that his fingernails were clearly seen and a jelly like substance was still pliable on the top of his head. The Nimerigar had dark brown wrinkled skin, a wide flat nose, low forehead, and a wide thin-lipped mouth.

The two prospectors took their little man to Casper. Once the news got out of their find, scientists and sideshow hunters flocked to the town. X-rays were performed and, despite many thinking it was a hoax, a full-grown adult skeleton was revealed. The X-rays also revealed his teeth were overly pointed. The little man had been killed violently with a blow to the head and he had spinal damage. The substance on the top of his head was congealed blood and brain tissue. The mummy went on a sideshow circuit for many years and later into private hands, finally disappearing.

The two prospectors went back to mining in the Pedro Mountains calling their claim the "Little Man Mine." They never did discover gold, but if you are near the Pedro Mountains look for the sign that shows you where the mine is located and watch out for the Nimerigar..now that you have proof they are real!

Laramie

Another town that sprung up around the railroad, Laramie is named after the French trapper Jacques LaRamie ,who disappeared in the Laramie Mountains in the late 1810s. The town is now a hotspot for outdoor enthusiasts.

Wyoming Territorial Prison

975 Snowy Range Road
Laramie, WY 82070
(307) 745-6161
www.wyomingterritorialpark.com

Built in 1872, the Wyoming Territorial Prison is the oldest and some say the best preserved prison in the west. Home for some of the west's most infamous outlaws including Butch Cassidy, Ellijah Canary, and Dan Parker, the prison also held twelve women and well above 1,000

Wyoming Territorial Penitentiary is the oldest and best preserved prison in the West, and it is currently occupied by the spirits of the former inmates. *Courtesy of Library of Congress.*

Visitors and employees often smell cigar smoke from one such *spirited* inmate.
Courtesy of Library of Congress.

men over the years. Due to overcrowding and poor facilities, the prison was closed in the summer of 1903 and inmates moved to a new facility in Rawlins. The compound was then turned into an experimental farm run by the University of Wyoming, housing sheep and cattle. In 1989, a small group of Laramie citizens rallied to have the building restored; in 1991, it was reopened as a prison, but the only inmates there now are the spirits of the past.

One of the prison's claim to fame is that it is the only prison facility to hold Butch Cassidy. In 1894, Butch was sentenced for stealing horses and spent only eighteen months of his two-year sentence. He was released early for good behavior and promising the governor he would leave Wyoming and never return.

Staff and visitors to the prison have reported several unexplained events... many of them are thought to be caused by the ghost of Julius Greenwald. Greenwald's was one of only two deaths that occurred within the prison's walls. He was incarcerated for murdering his wife Jennie in Evanston, Wyoming, in 1897. While incarcerated, the warden allowed him to make cigars, which was his trade prior to his arrest. He would sell the cigars to his fellow inmates. Unlike most ghosts, he was not murdered or killed by the guards; instead he died a natural death in 1901, of heart failure.

Many weird occurrences have been attributed to Greenwald's ghost: opening the gates of the prison forcefully despite the fact they are locked tight; icy spots felt all over the prison; and the smell of cigar smoke are common. Much to the fright of many, they have seen Greenwald's reflection in the window standing behind them. In 1991, two visitors on a tour of the prison noticed a man standing in the doorway near them; he was wearing prison clothing. After taking a double-take, the man had vanished. Later on the tour the visitors were looking at the inmates' photographs and recognized Greenwald as the man they had seen earlier.

During the Halloween season, the Wyoming Territorial Prison holds ghost tours, inviting you to take a walk in the haunted walls by candlelight.

Directions To Laramie Plains Civic Center: From Wyoming Territorial Prison, head south and turn left at West Garfield Street. Take the first left onto Snowy Ridge Road, continue onto West Clark Street, turn right at North 3rd Street, left at East Grand Avenue, right at South 7th Street, and then make the first left onto East Garfield Street.

Laramie Plains Civic Center

710 East Garfield Street
Laramie, WY 82070
(307) 745-8000
www.laramieplainsciviccenter.org

Rumors have surrounded the Laramie Plains Civic Center for many years. According to the stories, paranormal activity occurs all over the old school building. Employees claim that phones ring with no one on the other end, copiers turn on and off by themselves even after the equipment has been unplugged, and paperwork and office items go missing or are rearranged at night after everyone has left.

Over the years phantom footsteps have been heard walking the hallways and clouds of supernatural rose scented perfume detected. Doors have opened by an unseen hand and once an employee saw a dark-haired man wearing a yellow shirt sitting at the janitor's desk. Upon investigation, the man had disappeared and could not be found in the building.

SIGHTINGS

Indian Curse

The year was 1874 and two men were trying to win the heart of a half-breed Sioux maiden. Adolph Penio and Touinant Kensler were also Sioux half-breeds working at the same Laramie area ranch as the maiden. The maiden could only speak French and Penio was lucky enough to speak a bit of it. Kensler seemed to be out of luck, but quickly came up with a plan. He hired John Boyd to converse with the maiden on his behalf, but Boyd soon fell for the maiden as well.

Kensler had suspected for some time that Boyd was wooing the maiden for himself. On one drunken evening Kensler went looking for Boyd, but found the maiden girl in the arms of Penio. Outraged and out of his mind with jealously, Kensler shot the unsuspecting Penio through the window and ran off. When Kensler was questioned about the murder, he claimed Boyd had shot Penio, but Boyd, fortunately, had an alibi. Kensler was quickly convicted with help from Boyd's testimony and sentenced to hang for the murder of his rival Penio. The same day Kensler's sentence was announced, Boyd ran out and married the Indian maiden. Kensler was furious and exclaimed upon hearing the news, "My spirit will come back from the happy hunting grounds and John Boyd won't have good luck." On November 19, 1875, one year to the day that Kensler was hanged, John Boyd accidentally drowned in the North Platte River.

SIGHTINGS

Telephone Canyon

Some time not so long ago a weary traveler was trying to get home to Laramie taking the Lincoln Highway. It was late at night and he had not seen any cars along the road. It was also the middle of winter with sub-zero temperatures and a blizzard blaring. All of a sudden in his headlights was a man walking along the road. He pulled to the side of the road behind the man and quickly noticed the man only had a silk bomber jacket on. Surely he was freezing, the traveler thought. He had not noticed any ranches nearby or cars broken down. He rolled down his window and spoke quickly to the man. Immediately feeling comfortable with him, the traveler did not think twice about letting the man drive.

It wasn't long before the traveler fell asleep. When the car stopped, he awoke and noticed the stranger sitting motionless with his hands on the steering wheel, staring straight ahead. The stranger had driven the complete thirty-five miles through Telephone Canyon. The driver opened the door and got out. Assuming he was headed to a nearby ranch or into Laramie, the traveler asked if the stranger wanted to go on further to Laramie. The stranger quietly replied no and walked back down into the canyon.

The man really didn't think too much further about it. He was just glad that someone else drove the treacherous Telephone Canyon safely during the blizzard, which had now passed. The night sky was clear.

A few days later, the traveler spoke to a friend about his trip. Upon learning that the traveler had driven through Telephone Canyon, his friend wondered how that could be since he had to turn back due to the road's closure and stay in Casper. The traveler explained about the mysterious hitchhiker to his friend including what he was wearing. He had picked him up just outside of Casper and the man returned to the canyon once he got out. After a few minutes of silence, the traveler realized that the man looked exactly like himself.

(Author's note: Lincoln Highway was the first transcontinental route. Since it was created in 1913, the route has changed many times, as more direct routes were established. The road noted in the story is now a gravel road and it's not known if it is drivable.)

TRIP 2

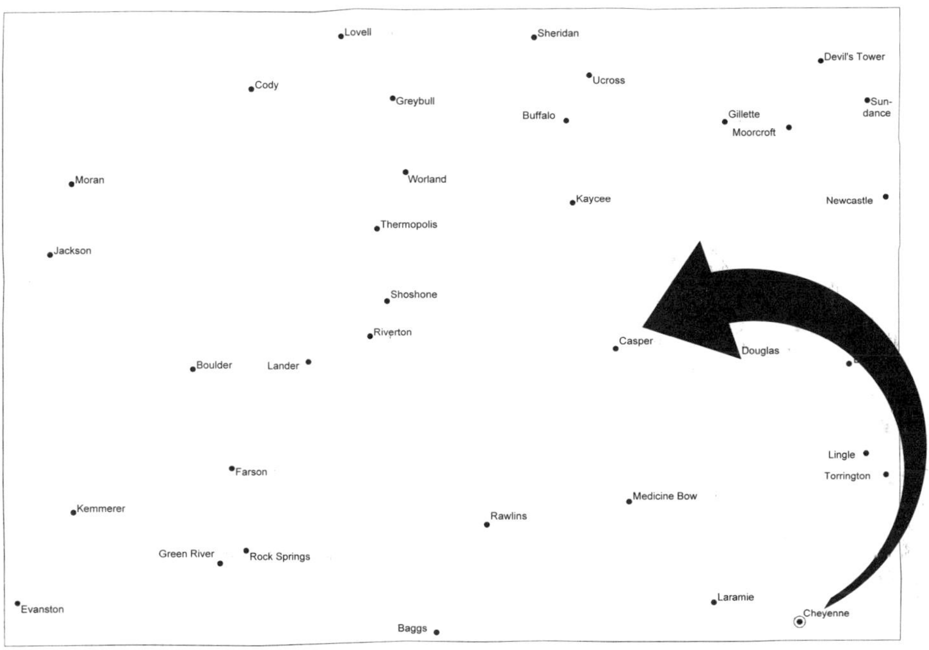

CHEYENNE TO CASPER

Cheyenne

Today Cheyenne is the largest town and the capital city of Wyoming. Plotted way back in 1867 as an encampment during the building of the railroad across Crow Creek, the town prospered even after the railroad was finished. Named after the prominent Great Plains tribe, Cheyenne is by far the most prominent town in Wyoming.

(Author's note: Cheyenne was very difficult to map out, so if you know a better route to the places in this chapter please take it.)

Terry Bison Ranch

51 I-25 Service Road East
Cheyenne, Wyoming 82007
(307) 634-4171

The Terry Bison Ranch encompasses nearly 30,000 acres in Wyoming and Colorado. Once land Ancient Indians called home, the Terry Bison Ranch now runs 2,000 bison and uses many of the original buildings from when the ranch was first established in the 1880s.

Francis Warren, the first Territorial Governor of Wyoming, purchased the ranch from Charles Terry in 1885. The Warren Livestock Company ran cattle, sheep, and bred sheepdogs. Many influential people were friends with the governor. President Theodore Roosevelt and General Pershing were known to visit frequently and General Pershing's son, Warren, worked at the Terry Ranch when he was on break from school at Harvard.

Nowadays you don't have to be influential to stay at the Terry Ranch or even work on the ranch unless, of course, if you want to. Today you can stay at the ranch in one of their many accommodations from bunkhouse rooms to single bedroom cabins. Even RV hookups are available for those who want to bring their own bed. The Senator's Steakhouse and Brass Buffalo Saloon offer everything from onion rings to Bison short ribs. Besides a place to rest your head and grab some grub, the Terry Bison Ranch offers activities from train rides to a bison hunt. It even has a ghost or two.

At the Senator's Steakhouse, employees and guests have reported items moving in the restaurant as well as lights turning on and off. One patron was even trapped in the bathroom when the door would not open.

The door does not have a lock on it and usually does not stick. Other women have complained that the stall doors slam repeatedly when they are using the restroom. However, the unusual activity is not just confined to the women's restroom; these occurrences have happened in the men's room as well, including one report that a picture banged against the wall repeatedly one evening.

An employee at the restaurant reported seeing a transparent little girl in the kitchen on the security camera. He was so spooked...he ran outside and waited for others to arrive for work before reentering the building. On another occasion the bartender was closing up the building for the night after the last of the guests left and saw a bright blue ball of light transcending the stairs. When it reached the bottom, it just dissipated. Other strange events have happened in the bar area as well: glasses fly off shelves and break and bartenders will feel a tapping on their shoulders and something brushing against them when no one is near.

Long-dead cowboys still reside in their bunkhouse at the Terry Bison Ranch.
Courtesy of Library of Congress.

The original bunkhouse is still in use for visitors to the ranch, but it seems the spirit of a cowboy may call the bunkhouse his home year round. Two cowboys working on the ranch were playing cards in one of the upstairs rooms when the losing cowboy accused the other of cheating. Of course, the other cowboy denied this and a fight broke out; ultimately one of the cowboys was killed in the skirmish. Guests and employees report the cowboy is still around, as sounds of heavy boots walking and voices are heard in the bunkhouse. People have even heard an argument coming from the upstairs when the bunkhouse is seemingly empty.

Other paranormal occurrences include the lights turning on and off by themselves, sheets that are tugged on when patrons are sleeping, and, from outside, people have seen the curtains move when the bunkhouse is vacant. A few of the ranch hands stayed the night in the bunkhouse and experienced the cowboy firsthand. In the beginning, they heard several voices talking and then the sound of boots walking across the floor. Finally the lights began to turn on and off. The men immediately jumped up and searched the bunkhouse, but no one else was there. They thought it best if they found another place to sleep.

Directions To Cheyenne Deming Elementary School: From the Terry Bison Ranch Resort, head south on Forest Service Road/703W and take the first right onto WY-210E/Happy Jack Road. Turn left onto I-80E towards Cheyenne; get off at Exit 358 and merge onto US-30E/West Lincoln Way. Turn right at Ames Avenue and then left at Deming Drive. Take the second right onto Snyder Avenue and then turn left at West 5th Street. *(On your way into the town of Cheyenne, the Francis E. Warren Air Base will be on your left. See sidebar.)*

Cheyenne Deming Elementary School

715 West 5th Avenue
Cheyenne, Wyoming 82001
(307) 771-2400
www.miller.laramie1.org

An innocent enough place is an elementary school. However, the Cheyenne Deming Elementary School is the site of a murder. Legends say if you look out the school windows at night you will see your reflection — and the murdered man's reflection standing next to you. Lights turn on and off by themselves and banging noises are heard throughout the building at night.

Directions to Havens Treasures Flea Market: From Cheyenne Deming Elementary School, head west on West 5th Street toward Reed Avenue and turn right onto Snyder Avenue. Turn left at Deming Drive. Take the first right onto Ames Avenue and then turn right at West Lincoln Way. Turn left at the Third Cross Street onto Thomes Avenue and then make the first right onto West 17th Street.

Francis E. Warren AFB

www.warren.af.mil

Just outside Cheyenne sits the oldest continuously active military installation. Fort D. A. Russell was established in 1867 and has been used for the U.S. Army Calvary during the Spanish-American War; it was not until 1930 that it took on its present name as the Francis E. Warren Air Force Base. Through the years many stories have surfaced about spirits that roam the fields and buildings of this base. Calvary soldiers still walk the halls of the dormitories and fall in line for formation in the fields.

The old administration building has several stories connected to it, ranging from an escaped insane asylum inmate killing nurses to a love story gone bad where one of the lovers was thrown out an upper window of the building. The Cheyenne Paranormal Team has investigated this building and reported several strange occurrences: at one point a compass started malfunctioning, cold spots were felt all over the building, batteries in their equipment would drain suddenly, and they even witnessed a door suddenly pop open by itself.

The old base hospital has reports of doors slamming, footsteps, cool breezes, and sounds of gurneys rolling down the hallways. The building is no longer used as a hospital and many of the staff members have seen apparitions, including cavalry officers and a young girl, in various areas.

The library was used as the infantry barracks when the fort was established. Several people have witnessed books that spontaneously fly off shelves. Perhaps the soldiers are not big fans of reading.

One of the Officers' Quarters houses has had several unnerving occurrences. The residents of this house report doors open and close, banging noises from the back of the house when no one is around, and on one scary occasion the residents went to check on their crying baby and found the bassinet swaying back and forth as if an unseen person was trying to console the infant. The Cheyenne Paranormal Team was also allowed to investigate this house, along with many of the other buildings, and found some surprising activity in the house. They heard doors slamming, but, upon investigation, could not find the source of the noise. They also witnessed a point of light on the servants' staircase; the light came from the corner of the wall and aimed straight at one of the investigators. The strange light then brushed up against the investigator and disappeared. The investigator said it felt like he got touched at that moment. At the same time, they had temperature fluctuations and other strange noises were heard.

Was It a UFO?

On a quiet night in 1976 two men were on-duty. To stay awake at night the men would listen to the Security Alert Teams (SAT) patrolling near one of the many missile sites near the Launch Control Facility. Around 2 a.m., they heard across the radio that two of the SAT should stop their vehicle and look around at the sky. A few seconds later an excited voice came across the radio claiming a white pulsating light was in the sky; between the pulsations the light would turn red and blue. The two men on-duty called to the SAT and asked what was going on. The SAT declared that a cigar shaped object with pulsating lights was moving around the sky near the Launch Control Facility. For the next couple of hours radio conversation continued between the two parties documenting the movement of the cigar shaped object. It seemed the object would move through the sky and stop briefly over or near the different missile silos. Each time the SAT would follow or get close to the object, they would have car problems and other electronic equipment difficulties. Around 4:30 that morning, the object quickly spirited off in the sky and disappeared.

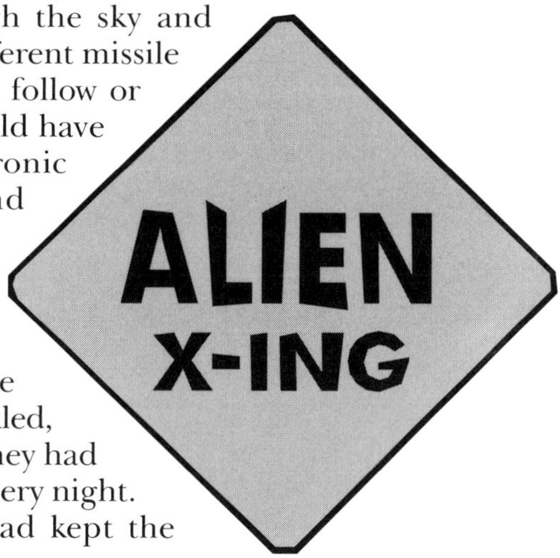

When this was reported to other launch control capsule commanders, many of them chuckled, but one came forward and said they had seen the same thing earlier that very night. Afraid to say anything, they had kept the incident quiet.

Havens Treasures Flea Market

312 West 17th Street
Cheyenne, Wyoming 82001
(307) 632-5330

Not too many years ago, while cleaning the stage area, a little trap door was revealed. Running to grab a flashlight, no one could have imagined what had been kept under the stage for so many years. Rummaging revealed some old photos and then a casket was found.

Thinking it was just a prop, the employee jumped back in horror — it contained a skeleton! Its dress tattered and hanging from the bones, a bit of the hair remained in the coffin. The skeleton turned out to be that of a teenage girl. Forgotten for so many years, none of the old-timers even knew of its existence.

Havens Treasures Flea Market occupies a building built for the Knights of Pythias. The Lodge was formed in Cheyenne in 1875 and to this day still holds meetings in its original building. The second floor is the Lodge's meeting hall, with businesses coming and going on the first floor. The building to the left was once joined to the Pythias Hall and still maintains the original look on the outside.

The Lodge Hall is where most of the unexplained events occur. Pictures, often found skewed, are returned to their position...only to be found crooked again. Knocks are heard coming from doors when no one is around. Furniture moving and footsteps have been heard in the main floor store from the second-story Lodge Hall. The basement, which is used to store the decorations for the annual Halloween haunted house, is also reported to be haunted by a spirit. Employees claim to hear a little girl's voice and feel tugging on their clothing when they are in the basement.

Directions To City News & Pipe Shop: From Havens Treasures, head northeast on West 17th Street and take the first left onto Carey Avenue.

City News & Pipe Shop

1722 Carey Avenue
Cheyenne, Wyoming 82001
(307) 638-8671

In downtown Cheyenne the City News & Pipe Shop is located in the corner of a building that was built in 1912. The Citizens Bank occupied the building until 1924. In 1925, H. N. Boyd purchased the building and turned the first floor into a drug store, cigar shop, and office spaces. The property underwent renovation in 1974 and got a new owner, who turned the property into what it is today — a bookstore, tobacco shop, and coffeehouse.

Employees at City News claim to experience paranormal activity just about every day. Each morning, as they are opening up the shop, the security system will beep until an employee greets the spirit. On other occasions, employees have heard sounds coming from children's books section; after they greet the spirit again with a 'good morning,' the sounds will stop.

After the resident spirit gets his morning greeting, sometimes "he" will stand behind the employees and whisper; other times "he" moves books around the store and occasionally slams doors.

The employees have concluded that the spirit must be the past doctor who held a practice in the building and may just be lonely. Perhaps he wants to talk to someone.

Directions To Cheyenne Atlas Theater: Head northwest on Carey Avenue toward West 18th Street. Take the First right onto Capital Avenue and then make the second right onto West 16th Street/West Lincoln Way.

Cheyenne Atlas Theater

211 West 16th Street
Cheyenne, Wyoming 82001
(307) 635-0199
www.cheyennelittletheatre.org

Built in 1885, the Atlas Theater has been home to many different types of businesses over the years, including a clothing store, a confectionery shop, a barber shop, and a furniture store. At one time it was even a hotel. In 1907, the first floor of the building was turned into The Atlas Theater, which changed its name to The Strand in 1929. In the 1950s the theater closed its doors; in 1961, it reopened as a nightclub. In 1971, the Cheyenne Little Theater Players bought the old Atlas Theater.

The theater troop are not the only ones to occupy this building. Several spirits have been reported to call it home too. One of the spirits is that of a woman wearing a dark Victorian era dress and hat. She has been seen in the upper floors and does not appear to know the living is occupying the building. Before the Atlas Theater was constructed, a tragic event happened on the block where the building now stands. Two of the buildings collapsed, killing two

Ghosts at the Atlas Theater still watch performances.
Courtesy of Library of Congress.

young boys while they slept in bed. The mother of these boys never recovered from their deaths, claiming she did not kiss them good night that evening. A gentleman was also crushed to death from the debris of the fallen building. Is the Victorian lady the mother of these boys still grieving their deaths? Another death, which did occur in the theater building, is of a man who shot himself in 1961 when the building was briefly used as a hotel.

Strange occurrences happen in the building all the time. On occasion

Employees of the Atlas Theater confirm how spirits often move scenery and stage props late at night. *Courtesy of Library of Congress.*

staff will unlock the building in the morning to find all the stage scenery have been moved, including the lights and other technical equipment. It appears the ghosts are putting on a play of their own... just a different kind of play than the living.

SIGHTINGS

Brownies

The Cherokee tell tales of little people who live in caves on the mountainside. The little people average knee height with long hair reaching the ground. These little people are known to be quite beautiful and, unlike the Nimerigar, they are kind souls. When the little people aren't helping people, they can be found singing, dancing, and playing music.

Known as Brownies, there are three different kinds of these little people: the Laurel people, Rock people, and Dogwood people. The Rock people are the malevolent ones — they throw rocks at people and have been known to steal children. The Laurel people are the mischievous ones — they like to play tricks on people and tell jokes. If you find your child laughing in their sleep, it is from the Laurel people chatting away the night. The Dogwood people are the nurturers, taking care of the sick and the lost.

Each of these little people can teach us lessons. The Rock people teach us about karma, the Laurel people teach us not to take the world too seriously, and the Dogwood people tell us to keep things simple and do kind acts out of the goodness of your heart.

Even though these little people are joyous, one should be cautious around them. Occasionally drumbeats can be heard in the mountains... do not approach or try to find the source of the music. The little people do not like to be disturbed at home. If they are, they will put a spell on the unwanted intruder, causing the intruder to enter a daze and lose his way. Sometimes at night they will come to harvest your crops. People have reported hearing the little people talking, but they dare not go outside. If you go outside to watch the little people gathering up your harvest, you will surely die. In the morning, you will find your harvest gathered in a pile in the center of your field.

If you are out in the woods and you find a knife or another trinket, be sure to ask the little people before you take it. You are welcome to talk out loud, even if you think the woods are empty. Be assured a little person is near enough to hear you. If you do not ask permission before taking the trinket, you will have stones thrown at you until you reach home. When you are out fishing and you think you caught the big one, but it turns out to only be a stick, it is the little people. If you are out walking in the woods and you see something out of the corner of your eye, that is the little people...keeping an eye on you.

Directions To Plains Hotel: From Cheyenne Atlas Theater, head southwest on West 16th Street/West Lincoln Way and take the first right onto Carey Avenue. Take the first right onto West 17th Street and then the second right onto Central Avenue.

Plains Hotel

1600 Central Avenue
Cheyenne, Wyoming 82001
(866) 275-2467
www.theplainshotel.com

In June 1910, construction of the Plains Hotel commenced. The hotel started out as an offhand remark by Thomas Heaney, the president of the Industrial Club (Chamber of Commerce). The main hotel in town was outdated and had turned into more of a bar than the luxury hotel Cheyenne so badly needed. In March 1911, the hotel hosted its grand opening and it was quite the party; men and women dressed in their finest duds and the band played all night long.

The new hotel had five floors carpeted in velvet, three elevators, and one hundred elegant rooms that contained private baths, telephones, and the finest furniture money could buy. It even had an orchestra on staff to entertain guests as they milled through the hotel's lobby.

Honeymooners checked in quite frequently, but one couple never left. Rosie was a glowing bride excited about the start of her new life with her handsome husband. One evening, after checking in, Rosie went looking for her husband who had not returned to their room. She spotted him in the hotel bar speaking with an unsuspecting woman. Rosie hid just out of sight and, when her husband followed the woman upstairs, she followed also. In the woman's room, she caught her new husband and the woman together and, in a rage, she shot them both. Rosie then returned to her room; distraught, she shot herself.

Rosie and her husband have been seen at the hotel, but don't forget about the other woman. She too sticks around the hotel even after death. Housekeeping has heard loud sobbing coming from Rosie's room; upon investigation, no one is found and the sobbing stops abruptly when the door is opened. Rosie has been seen wearing a long blue gown on the second floor of the hotel.

Rosie's husband roams the hotel dressed in a long black tail suit and white shirt with a silver button at the top. He is seen most often on the fourth floor, but glimpses of him have been seen all over the hotel.

The woman from the bar is seen on the second floor, wearing a short red dress. One Halloween the hotel set up two mannequins; one as a bride and one as the groom. One staff member saw a woman wearing a short red dress just behind the bride mannequin...suddenly the bride crashed to the floor! Just as quickly as "she" fell, the woman in red disappeared.

Another spirit also inhabits the Plains Hotel. Not much is known about this spirit except it is thought an argument broke out between two guests and, during the fight, one guest pushed the other; subsequently one of the guests lost their balance and fell out the window. The man fell four floors to his death. His poor soul remains at the hotel...locked into an eternal fight on the fourth floor.

SIGHTINGS

Underground Tunnel

Today the tunnels are closed to the public. Though occasionally portions are opened for tours, be assured they are down there beneath the streets as you walk above. The tunnels were developed to conceal the steam pipes that would heat the city, but after the steam plant closed down the tunnels were abandoned and started crumbling. If you are lucky enough to gain entrance to some of the older buildings and hotels, you can still see the archways that led to the tunnels.

A few lucky ones who have made it down into the tunnels claim to have had some spooky experiences. Voices and heavy footsteps made from boots have been heard from parts of the tunnels that are inaccessible. What or who is down in the tunnels we may never know, but while you are aboveground remember that ghosts may be following you...underground.

Directions To St. Mark's Episcopal Church: From the Plains Hotel, head southeast on Central Avenue toward East 16th Street/East Lincoln Way. Take the first left onto Warren Avenue, the second left onto East 18th Street, and turn right at the second cross street onto Capital Avenue. Turn right onto West 19th Street, right onto Central Avenue, right onto West 18th Street, and right onto Capital Avenue. Turn right at the third cross street onto West 21st Street and then take the first right onto Central Avenue.

St. Mark's Episcopal Church

1908 Central Avenue
Cheyenne, Wyoming 82001
(307) 634-7709
www.stmarkscheyenne.org

In 1888, St. Mark's Episcopal Church was finished enough to hold services for its congregation. The belltower was the only part of the church that needed to be finished, and it would take nearly thirty years to complete.

Two Swedish men were hired to complete the tower, but when it was forty feet tall the men mysteriously disappeared. The church hired new workers to finish the project, but they had problems concentrating on

Are two workmen trapped in the belltower at St. Mark's Episcopal Church?
Courtesy of Library of Congress.

their task when strange sounds and voices started coming from the tower. The men complained of ghostly hammering and tapping. Nonetheless, they finished the tower in 1924.

Many years later a man revealed the fate of the two Swedish workers, explaining that one of the workers slipped and fell to his death in the tower. His friend panicked, thinking he would be deported, or worse, entombed with his friend in the tower's walls and fled.

A psychic claimed to sense two spirits in the tower. One was the worker who fell to his death and the other is that of Father Rafter, who was in charge of the church at the time of the man's death. Other visitors to the church have claimed to hear the church's pipe organ playing when no one is around it, voices within the walls of the belltower, and the church bells occasionally ringing of their own accord. Is Father Rafter summoning his congregation, or is it the unfortunate worker calling for help?

Directions to Edwin Smalley House: Head southeast on Central Avenue, toward East 19th Street, and take the first left onto Warren Avenue. Turn right at the third cross street onto East 22nd Street.

Edwin Smalley House

624 East 22nd Street
Cheyenne, Wyoming 82001
Private residence

Edwin J. Smalley is best known for his role in arresting Tom Horn, the Pinkerton detective and later murderer, in 1901. Edwin and his wife Edith lived in the house until his death in 1937; Edith remained on there until 1940. The Smalley house then changed hands several times and eventually had a string of renters residing there. In 1988, the house again became a private residence.

A little girl named 'Amy' has been seen and heard all over the Smalley house. She appears to children most often, but likes to show herself to adults as well. Amy appears to be thirteen or fourteen years old with blond hair. Occasionally you can catch a glimpse of her looking out one of the upstairs windows. Residents and visitors to the house have also reported hearing several different voices holding conversations. Objects move around the house or disappear completely. Occasionally residents will hear loud thumping or unexplained banging coming from unoccupied rooms; upon investigation nothing is out of place.

No one is sure who the little girl is or why she remains in the house. Is she responsible for the objects moving or is it another spirit altogether?

Directions To Eloxite Company: From the Edwin Smalley House, head southwest on East 22nd Street toward Maxwell Avenue. Turn right at Warren Avenue, left at US-85 N/Central Avenue, and then merge onto I-25N via the ramp to Torrington/Wheatland. Take Exit 78 toward I-25 BUS/Wheatland; turn right at West Mariposa Parkway, left at 16th Street, right at Maple Street, and left at 10th Street.

Wheatland

Not much is known about the town of Wheatland, but the Wyoming State license place features a bucking horse called Steamboat that was stabled in a barn in Wheatland.

Eloxite Company

806 10th Street
Wheatland, Wyoming 82201
(307) 322- 3050
www.eloxite.com

Eloxite Company is a wholesale jewelry company that had a brush with the supernatural. According to reports in the late 1970s, the company acquired an Indian Skull that was unearthed from western Iowa. The plan was to display the skull in the front of the store where a small museum was set up showcasing artifacts and unusual rocks.

A few years went by and the museum part of the store closed down; the skull was boxed up and moved to the basement for storage. It was not long before the skull started protesting its new home.

The activity started almost immediately... According to staff members, after hearing "a big crash," they found several boxes on the ground including the box with the skull in it. The employees replaced all the items to the storage rack and went back to their chores.

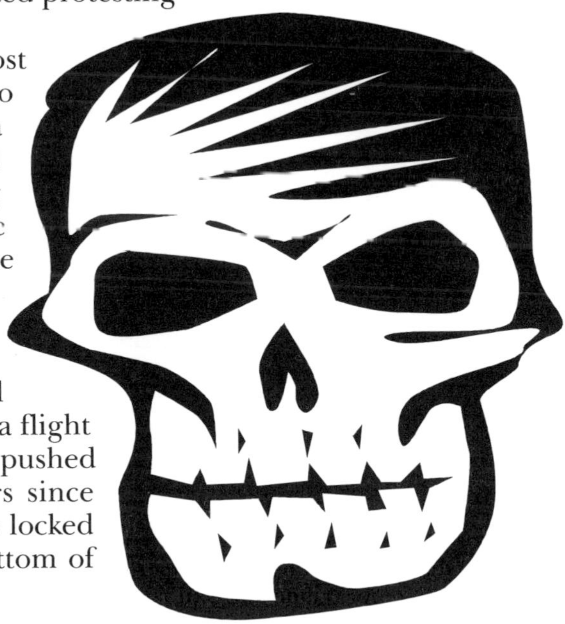

The next noise that occurred resulted in several suitcases being thrown down a flight of stairs. No one could have pushed the suitcases down the stairs since the door above the stairs was locked ... as was the door at the bottom of the stairs.

Other objects started flying off the walls, including expensive paintings. The activity increased, each day getting worse. Finally, as a few employees were walking in a corridor in the basement, a crowbar flew out in front of them, bouncing a few times until it came to a rest at their feet. This was the final straw — the owners had to figure out what was going on.

Suspecting the activity was from the skull, the owners contacted a mortuary in Council Bluffs, Iowa. Luckily, the mortuary was more than happy to rebury the skull in an Indian Burial Ground near Council Bluffs and, since the skull was buried in 1984, no activity has been reported.

Did the skull get upset that it had been put into storage with all the other artifacts? No one will ever know for sure the reason the skull had for knocking over boxes and disrupting the shop, but since the skull has been laid to rest in Iowa all has been quiet at the jewelry store.

Directions To Fort Laramie: From Eloxite Company, head south on 10th Street toward Maple Street and take the first left onto 9th Street. Continue onto Swanson Road and turn right to merge onto I-25N toward Douglas; from I-25 take Exit 92 to U.S. Highway 26, proceed east to the town of Fort Laramie, turn right on State Highway 160, and travel three miles to the park entrance.

Fort Laramie

965 Gray Rocks Road
Fort Laramie, Wyoming 82212
(307) 837-2221
www.nps.gov/fola/index.html

Every seven years a woman riding a black stallion and wearing a green dress is seen outside the fort. She is the oldest spirit at Fort Laramie. Legend states she was an officer's daughter who enjoyed riding outside of the fort, despite her father's concerns. One day she went out for a ride and never returned — and neither she nor her body were ever found. In 1971, a young lieutenant, James Nicolas Allison, saw the woman riding. After inquiring about her, he learned of the stories that had been floating around for nearly twenty years prior. Her next ride will be in 2011.

One of the workmen at the Fort took a picture of the Old Bedlam building and, after looking at them on his computer, he noticed a person on the porch. He remembers that it was an early foggy day and no one was there at the time. Is this the ghost of a solider still keeping watch over the fort?

In the Officers' Quarters reports of lights burning late at night have been reported. The only problem is no electricity runs to that building. Are late-night meetings taking place? Perhaps the spirits that remain within the fort just can't sleep.

Spirits roam the grounds of Fort Laramie. *Courtesy of Library of Congress.*

Lights and ghostly figures have been seen inside the Calvary Barracks at Fort Laramie late at night. *Courtesy of Library of Congress.*

On another day the same maintenance man was working in a building doing some plastering with a co-worker when he was overcome with the smell of rose water, a perfume common in the 1800s. He looked up at his co worker who had a strange look on his face; they both quickly got up and left the building. Returning fifteen minutes later, the smell had vanished.

Fort Laramie started in 1834 as a trading post, and was originally called Fort John. In 1849, the United States Army purchased the fort and began a military outpost. The soldiers patrolled the Oregon Trail to ensure the protection of the travelers against Indians. Later the fort became a depot for the Pony Express, Overland Stage, and the Transcontinental Telegraph System.

Like most forts of the time, this fort was not walled in. Money and plans had been set aside to build a wall, but was never implemented. In 1934, the fort became a historical landmark.

Directions To Lusk: From Fort Laramie, head northeast on WY-160. Turn right at US-26E and then left at US-85N. *(Author's note: The first location in the next chapter is potentially dangerous to enter, so I did not include directions to it for your safety. The directions are only for the town of Lusk.)*

Lusk

Only holding a population of just over a thousand, Lusk hasn't changed much since its founding in 1886. The town is most famous for being located near the only monument given to a prostitute.

HOTEL The Yellow Hotel

Mary Ada Fisher followed the gold boom west from Ohio. After the gold dried up, she found herself in Casper following oil riches. Soon, the thirty-year-old prostitute found herself in the town of Lusk; the year was 1919. She later admitted she thought the town was called "Lust," but stayed nonetheless. Mary changed her name to Dell Burke, set up a tent, and started taking customers. Soon she had enough money to rent a house and bring in a few girls; it seemed Dell was on her way to bigger things. It was only a year later she bought a large house, painted it yellow, and took in even more girls. When she would acquire a new girl, she would fix them up and send them out to stroll the streets with Dell's signature poodle in their arms. This let the townspeople know that she had new 'merchandise.'

Dell entertained most of the towns' prominent citizens, and her house offered the "best steaks in Wyoming" where they could also dance to a live orchestra, play billiards and card games, and drink the finest booze around. Dell was well-respected even by the ladies of the town; she had a reputation for being quite generous. The madam put at least two boys through college, donated money to many of the charities in town, and would anonymously give money to citizens who were down on their luck. Dell sealed her position in the community when, in 1929, Lusk's Power and Water needed to immediately replace an engine and generator that kept the town running. Lusk was having problems financing the $22,300 needed, so Dell stepped in and loaned the town the finances to keep Lusk afloat. In the spring of 1930, the Sixth Judicial District Court tried to close Dell's business, but she held the upper hand and threatened to shut down the town's water and power literally.

Dell Burke's success allowed her to invest in property and other endeavors. She stayed in business during Prohibition, the Great Depression, and World War II. It was not until in 1978 that the last paying customer visited the Yellow Hotel. Dell fell on the sidewalk in front of her house a year later and broke her hip. She spent the next few years in a hospital care center until she finally passed away in 1980.

The Yellow Hotel now sits vacant, a little run down; the bright yellow paint fading in the hot Wyoming sun. Visitors to the house claim feeling a bit strange and overwhelmed while in the building. Some have even reported the smell of perfume floating through the rooms, seemingly following you around the house. Outside the house residents claim to have seen lights and hear music coming from the house long after Dell's death. Are these just memories of all the fun that went on in the house, or is it Mary Ada Fisher returning home?

Directions To Glenrock Paleontological Museum: From Lusk, continue on I-25/US 20W and take Exit 160 to merge onto US-20W toward Glenrock. Your destination will be on the left.

SIGHTINGS

Jackalope

Some say that the Jackalope is a legend; others say it is a real animal. The Jackalope is said to run at nearly ninety miles an hour and weigh only three to five pounds. Brown in color, it is a cross between a pygmy deer and a species of a killer rabbit. The vicious breed of rabbit has been dubbed the 'Warrior Rabbit' over the years due to its defense tactics. The rabbits have an uncanny way of mimicking human sounds and when the cowhands are out in the wilderness at night singing their campfire songs the jackalopes are often heard mimicking their voices. The animals only mate during thunderstorms and their milk is considered to be an aphrodisiac, but I dare anyone to try and milk a Jackalope. One way to see a Jackalope is to put out a bit of whiskey as it is reported to be the rabbit's favorite drink. The Jackalope has been seen all across the American West, but most sightings have been in Wyoming.

The first reports of Jackalopes started in the sixteenth century and since then many artists and writers have documented the mystical animal throughout the centuries. In Germany, they are known as the Wolperdinger or the Rasselbock. Switzerland calls the animal "Dildapp," and in Sweden, they are called the Skvader.

Some rabbits contract the virus Papillomatosis, a disease that has been dubbed "Jackalopism." When the rabbits contract this disease, their heads harden to such a point that sometimes horns are formed. However, the disease does not make the rabbits fast or cause them to mimic human voices.

In 1939, Douglas Herrick came home from hunting. Catching only a rabbit, he threw the carcass into his garage. The rabbit slid across the floor and came to rest against a pair of deer antlers. Douglas's brother Ralph exclaimed, "Look at that rabbit with horns on it!" Douglas, who was a taxidermist, mounted the antlers on the rabbit and the legend was born. Since that day in the garage, Jackalopes can be found all over: mounted on walls, on postcards, glasses, and other novelty items.

If you are still on the fence about Jackalopes, visit Douglas, Wyoming, and pick up a hunting license for one. There are a few stipulations that go along with hunting for one of these mystical creatures. The first rule is that you cannot have an IQ higher than 72 and you can only hunt the animals between midnight and 2 a.m. on June 21st. You may ask if anyone has ever caught a Jackalope... Just visit Douglas, Wyoming, and see for yourself.

To attract a Jackalope, set out a shot of whiskey.

Glenrock

Starting out as a stage stop along the Oregon Trail, Glenrock really made it big when oil was discovered nearby. However, Glenrock is most remembered for a nearby train wreck that killed nearly half of the train's sixty-six passengers in 1923, which was and still is the worst train accident in Wyoming's history.

Glenrock Paleontological Museum

506 West Birch Street
Glenrock, Wyoming 82637
(307) 436-2667
www.paleon.org

Built in 1918, the Glenrock Paleontological Museum is housed in the Bronco Building. Built next to the Hotel Higgins, the hotel was quickly rethought and the space was rented out to a number of businesses including *The Glenrock Independent*, the local newspaper. The editor of the newspaper and his family lived upstairs. Small businesses came and went until finally a car dealership took over the bottom floor, with the upstairs becoming apartments. Today the upstairs apartments hold no tenants except for the spirits that reside there while the first floor is home to the Glenrock Paleontological Museum.

Staff at the museum claim all sorts of different phenomena happen in the building. Lights flare bright and then go back to normal and electronic devices go off for no reason. Phantom footfalls have been heard in the education room. An apparition has been seen in the basement of the building as well as unexplained noises heard throughout the building. It seems that more than just dinosaur bones hang around the Bronco Building.

Directions to Higgins Hotel: From Glenrock Paleontological Museum, head west on West Birch Street toward South 5th Street. Your destination will be on the right.

Higgins Hotel

417 Birch Street
Glenrock, Wyoming 82637
(307) 436-9212
www.higginshotel.com

Reports of paranormal activity have plagued the Higgins Hotel for years. Built in 1916 by John Higgins, a prominent citizen of Glenrock, the hotel quickly became the social center for the town. John Higgins had a volatile relationship with his wife who later met a mysterious death when she fell from her husband's motorcar. She was an eccentric woman and her death was never fully explained.

Through the years the hotel held secret poker games and meetings in the basement and some of the small rooms were later turned into apartments. The third-floor brass beds are original to the hotel as is most of the furnishings.

Employees refuse to enter the basement alone, claiming that a foreboding feeling comes over them as they descend the stairs. Shadows and apparitions have been seen throughout the hotel. Room 302 has quite a reputation for guests checking out abruptly or just flat out refusing to stay in the room.

Many guests claim a woman comes in their room at night to check on them and occasionally sits on their bed as they sleep. Other guests claim

to see a glimpse of a petticoat ascend the staircase. Cigarette smoke is smelled in the lobby even when no one is around... Is this the spirit of a past guest lighting up in another dimension?

The hotel also is home to the Paisley Shawl Restaurant & The Highlander Pub. This is where most of the activity has been reported. Candles are extinguished only to relight by an unseen presence, chairs and tableware move on their own accord, and whispers are heard throughout the dining area apparently coming from a woman who is no longer of this earthly plane. A newspaper reporter published a photo taken in the dining room of an apparition a few years back; whether this is an adulterated photo is still up for debate. Nonetheless photos taken in the room have revealed many unexplained anomalies.

A few years back the current owners of the hotel found a trunk in the basement full of a Victorian woman's belongings including a feather duster. Some think this trunk belongs to the resident ghost — a former housekeeper at the hotel — but is she the only spirit there? Others claim Mrs. Higgins still watches over the hotel, as well as a host of other long-dead guests and residents. In 1925, a nearby train crash killed twenty-five people... did those spirits find their way to the hotel after death? No one will ever know for sure who haunts the Higgins Hotel, but rest lightly, for the long-dead keepers of the hotel will check on you after you have gone to bed.

Directions To Ivy House Inn: From Higgins Hotel, head west on US-20. Turn left at South Wolcott Street, right at East 9th Street, and then take the third right onto South Ash Street.

Casper

The second largest city in Wyoming, Casper is the previous site of Fort Caspar, a trading post for the Oregon Trail. Casper has a long history in oil and is rich in cowboy history.

Ivy House Inn

815 South Ash
Casper, Wyoming 82601
(307) 268-8356
www.ivyhouseinn.com

Everything seemed quiet in the Ivy House Inn when the Johnsons bought the house...until the renovations started.

The one hundred-year-old house was owned by Mrs. White, who did the best she could with the house, often paying friends to do repair work with cookies. She is said to be controlling and manipulating even after her death. The house was built in 1902 and was occupied by more than twenty-five different families until the Whites' bought the house in 1940. The house was finally completed when the Whites added the porches in 1940. Mrs. White lived alone in the house with her two Siamese cats after her husband's death, finally passing away there in 1995.

Renovations started right away. Apparently Mrs. White wanted the new owners to be aware she was still in charge and was a bit unhappy with all the changes going on in her home. Drills would come unplugged, hammers would actually *get up and walk out* of rooms, and on one occasion, several 2 x 4's flew across a room at the new owner.

The new owner's dog also refused to enter certain rooms, including the basement. Strange unexplainable smells would come and go with no explanation, including rotting fish, burnt rubber, and baby powder. All these strange events prompted the Johnsons to start snapping pictures. To their surprise, the pictures revealed vortexes, strange mists, faces, and even apparitions and anomalies that could not be explained away by light, hair, camera straps, or any other natural phenomena.

Mrs. White has appeared on several occasions. Once during a dinner party she appeared to a woman in the bathroom. Another time she was seen powdering her nose, and simply walking down the hallway.

Mrs. White isn't the only spirit to occupy the house: a young man with a crew cut has been seen as well, wearing a flannel shirt, and carrying wood boards. This young man is thought to be a residual haunting. He always walks the same path and does not seem to notice anyone who might be in his way or in the room.

Many people have experienced phantom ghostly animals as well. Small cat-like figures have been seen running down the halls. Meows have been heard when no cats are around and mysterious scratching sounds are heard all over the house.

Directions To The Wonder Bar: From Ivy House Inn Bed and Breakfast, head north on South Ash Street toward West 8th Street. Turn right at the first cross street onto West Midwest Avenue and then take the second left onto South Center Street.

SIGHTINGS

Salt Creek Ghost Lights

Since the early 1900s ghosts lights have been reported near the Salt Creek Oil Field. Mr. O'Rourke was an Irish immigrant who came to the Wyoming territory to farm. Ever since his death his spirit has been seen in the area holding his old oil lantern, which he used to carry to check on his fields and livestock late at night. Farmers in the area have tried to catch the light, but as they approach the light always seems just out of reach. Occasionally the light will disappear and reappear farther off in the distance.

Many theories surround this light. Some think the light is natural gas escaping from the oil fields while others think it is a natural phenomena caused by squeezing of the minerals during small earthquakes and plate movement. Whatever the cause — ghost, gas, or minerals — it seems to be another mystery that remains unsolved. I like to believe it is the spirit of Mr. O'Rourke.

SIGHTINGS

Alien Baby

Several years back an interesting article surfaced in the *Weekly World News*: "Space Alien Baby Found!" Many of you may raise an eyebrow and chuckle a little. All government parties involved have denied the news story and the rancher that found the baby is not listed in the phone book or online. However, as with many unknown and unexplained events that have slipped through the cracks, i.e., Roswell 1947, government cover-ups are common.

According to the published account, the night prior to the alien discovery strange lights were seen in the area. After hearing a strange humming sound emanating from his barn on May 7, 2003, the rancher, Marleson, went to investigate and found a small creature on the floor of his barn.

Marleson's wife Cynthia took several photographs and a video of this creature, which was described as a scaly skinned infant. According to the paper, the infant had two brains, three hearts, and despite being quite thin was in good health. The infant could also produce, when aggravated, high-frequency wails capable of shattering glass.

After finding the infant, Marleson phoned the police and within an hour of the phone call, FBI agents started arriving. Donned in Hazardous Material suits, the men took the infant away and sealed off the area.

Whether this story is true or not, it is up for debate, but reports of alien babies seem to pop up all over the Internet and in tabloids. Are these all fabricated stories or is there some truth to it?

SIGHTINGS

Ship of Death

Next time you are walking along the Platte River near Casper beware of the "Ship of Death." Reports surface of a phantom ship that rises out of the mist on fall days. A massive rolling fog surrounds the ship and its crew. Covered in frost, the ship slowly sails by, with the crew huddled around a corpse laying silently on a canvas cloth. The crew slowly picks up the corpse, revealing to you the deceased, and then, slowly, the fog-covered ship sails by and vanishes as quickly and mysteriously as it came.

Victor Heibe was out working on the riverfront in the fall of 1903, when out of nowhere came the ship. He had heard the stories of others who had seen the ship and was terrified when he saw the corpse — it was his good friend! Later that day his friend passed away... It seems the ship always reveals its corpse and it's either a relative or friend of the viewer. Unfortunately, the corpse that is revealed always dies that same day.

Other documented accounts exist of the "Ship of Death." The first sighting was in 1862: a trapper looking to see if he had caught any beaver that day spotted the ship. The corpse was the trapper's fiancée; she died later that day. Gene Wilson saw the ship as he was out checking on his cattle. The year was 1887, and his wife died later that day.

THE WONDER BAR

256 South Center Street
Casper, Wyoming 82601
(307) 234-4110
www.thewonderbar.com

Advertised as Casper's Oldest Neighborhood Bar and Grill, The Wonder Bar started in the 1940s.Patrons used to ride their horses right up into the bar and order a beer. Today you can still bring your horse into the bar, but you need to make sure that your horse is potty-trained.

The street on which The Wonder Bar is located is known as Saloon Row. Over the years many bars have taken up residence on this famous street. The first bar to stake its claim was The Mint Bar opening in 1933; it served Near Beer during prohibition. The next year The Wonder Bar took over The Mint Bar after the repeal of prohibition. The bar became a popular place for locals and celebrities alike; Earnest Hemmingway even had a drink at the bar.

Being the oldest bar in Casper, it should come as no surprise that The Wonder Bar has a spirit or two of the non-drinking kind. A former employee has seen on occasion an apparition walking down the stairs of the building. Through the years, stories have arisen of paranormal happenings at the bar, including strange sounds heard all over the building and lights in the basement turning on and off.

The White Devil protects the wild Mustangs of Wyoming. *Courtesy of Bigstock Photos*

SIGHTINGS

Rattlesnake Range

The White Devil has protected the wild mustangs since cowboys started capturing them in the wild. This magnificent white stallion would attack the cowboys and, if the stallion got close enough, the animal would kick and bite at you. The stallion is still seen in the area even though wild mustangs are no longer wrangled.

TRIP 3

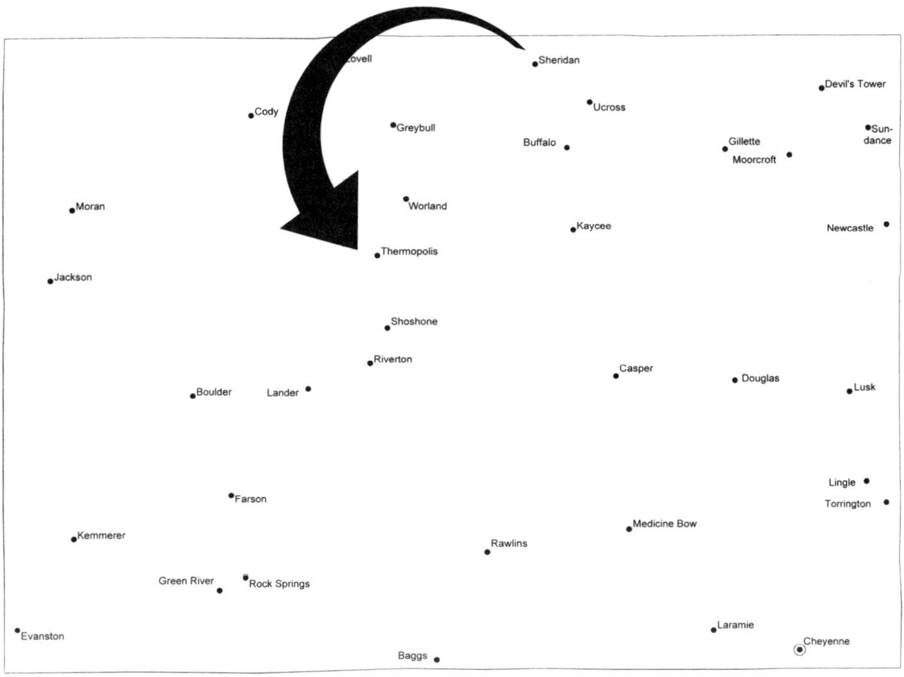

SHERIDAN TO THERMOPOLIS

SIGHTINGS

Lake De Smet

Located in the Northeast corner of Wyoming, the beautiful Lake De Smet has more to offer the recreationalist than one would think. Prior to the lake's enlargement into a reservoir, it was the largest natural body of water in northern Wyoming. Its shores remain in its natural state with wildlife roaming freely along the sloping hills that nestle the lake.

The Crow Indian tribe believe that Lake De Smet is home to a lake monster. Rising from the mist, the slimy snake-like creature searches for food. Early settlers to the area claimed their horses and dogs would not go near the water. Boaters and fishermen were reported missing after going to the lake. The lake monster is known to make a low, deep moaning sound from the depths of the lake. Today the Moaning Man Monster is still blamed for the missing men, women, and animals who venture too near to the lake.

SIGHTINGS

Devils Tower

A legend among the Indian tribes of the area near the Devils Tower has been told and retold through the ages:

> Seven young Indian maidens were playing in the forest when they came across a great bear. The bear gave chase and as the girls ran through the forest the bear quickly approached. Desperate the girls jumped up on

Many legends surround this great Wyoming landmark. *Courtesy of Library of Congress.*

> a rock and began to pray loudly to the Great Spirit to save them from the bear. Immediately the rock began to grow upwards toward the sky. Higher and higher, the bear desperately jumped against the side of the rock scratching at its sides, leaving deep claw marks in the rock. The rock continued to grow up to the heavens, the girls still on top became the seven stars of the Pleiades.

Today the rock is a popular climbing attraction. Devils Tower was first climbed on July 4, 1893 using a long wooden ladder attached to the rock face. President Theodore Roosevelt proclaimed the tower the first United States National Park in 1906. The Devils tower juts 1267 feet above the relatively flat landscape that surrounds it. The rock formation was used in the popular 1977 film Close Encounters of the Third Kind, and even though that was just a movie, for centuries and even today strange lights and UFOs have been seen flying around the tower's summit.

Sheridan

Established in 1882, Sheridan started as a cattle town. Cattle barons flocked to this little town and built it into the historical gem it is today.

Sheridan Inn

856 North Broadway
Sheridan, Wyoming 82801
(307) 637-2777
www.sheridaninn.com

The Burlington & Missouri Railroad and the Sheridan Land Company, providing rooms and food for businessmen coming out west, built the house of "69 Gables," as Ripley's Believe It or Not calls the hotel. In 1894, the hotel became home to Buffalo Bill Cody until 1902. Cody used to sit on the porch and audition hopeful showmen for his Wild West Show.

Miss Kate still loves to take care of the Sheridan Inn, which is haunted by more than just long-deceased cowboys. *Courtesy of Library of Congress.*

Sheridan Inn. *Courtesy of Library of Congress.*

Today the historic hotel offers guests twenty-two rooms, each named after one of Cody's friends or associations with his traveling Wild West Show. Each of the rooms contain a "mini museum" of the person it is named after.

The historic bar, 1893 Grille & Spirits, invites you to step back in time. Containing the original bar, you too could sit where Buffalo Bill Cody sat — third stool from the left. At that time the bar was solely for men, as proper women did not frequent bars. Horses on the other hand were commonplace. Many horses entered the bar after local races to a nearby town and back.

The main spirit that inhabits the hotel is of a woman who had many duties. She started her position at the inn and lived on-site until her death. "Miss Kate" loved the inn and was everything from a waitress and maid to a seamstress and caretaker. She is known to turn on and off the lights and make sounds, including knocking. If a fire is about to break out in the kitchen, she will set off the fire alarm to alert the present day staff. The kitchen staff report this has happened on many occasions.

Miss Kate requested she be cremated and her ashes placed in her room upon her death. It is said that an urn containing Miss Kate was placed behind the wall in her bedroom to always remain in the place she loved most. Her original furniture, including her favorite rocking chair, is still in her room. On occasion witnesses have seen Miss Kate rocking away silently or just the empty chair rocking slowly by itself.

Buffalo Bill frequented this Sheridan Inn bar, which he still likes to hang out at even after death. His favorite spot is the third stool to the left. *Courtesy of Library of Congress.*

Some of the other spirits you may run across at the inn is of the builder, who shot himself at the inn, the son-in-law of Buffalo Bill Cody, and an unknown little girl, who tugs on guests clothing or is seen skipping merrily down hallways.

Directions To Kendrick Mansion: From Sheridan Inn, head south on Broadway Street. Take the first right onto East 4th Street, the second right onto North Main Street, the first left onto West 5th Street, and then turn left at Clarendon Avenue.

Kendrick Mansion

400 Clarendon Ave
Sheridan, Wyoming 82801
(307) 674-4589
www.trailend.org

Built in 1913, Trails End was a showpiece of wealth and accomplishment for John Kendrick and his cattle business. He grew up a penniless orphan and wanted to show the world that he had finally made it. John's stay in the mansion was short-lived even though the Kendrick family would enjoy life at Trails End. Just a year after the mansion was completed John was elected governor of Wyoming and two years later he was elected to the United States Senate. John found success as a senator and was reelected repeatedly until in 1933. After becoming ill, he slipped into a coma and died a few days later. John finally returned to Trails End, but only to be the guest of honor at his funeral.

John's wife, son, and daughter spent quite a bit of time at Trails End. When Manfield (John's son) brought home his new wife, there was talk of moving out, but, after pressure from Manfield's mother, the couple stayed in the house raising two sons there until 1960. Rosa-Maye (John's daughter) loved Trails End and returned home as often as she could, but after marrying an Army Officer, she would spend time all over the world with her husband and would rarely return home. Finally, Eula, John's wife enjoyed the social life of being a senator's wife in Washington D.C., but relished the home her husband built and only moved out of it a few years before her death in 1961 to be close to her daughter in Texas.

The mansion is nearly 14,000 square feet and cost roughly $165,000. During its construction, a carriage house was built to house the Kendrick family. The carriage house was completed in 1910 and is 3,000 square feet. Situated on 3.8 acres of gardens, the mansion and surroundings are open to the public for self-guided tours or you can request a guided tour. Most of the original furnishings are still in the house, which often features temporary exhibits.

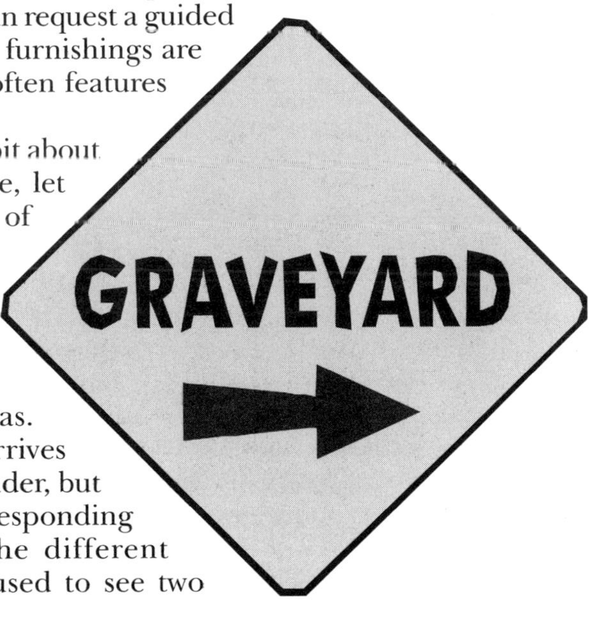

Now that you know a bit about the people and the house, let me tell you about some of the hauntings reported there. The mansion has surveillance cameras set up and, over the years, people have been seen late at night on these cameras. The police department arrives expecting to find an intruder, but no one is there. As the responding officer goes through the different rooms, he is often confused to see two people walking through the mansion...yet the officer claims he is the only one there. The spirits at Trails End seem to be curious about the people who visit the mansion. It is obvious the Kendrick family love Trails End even after death.

Directions To Kane: From Kendrick Mansion, head northeast on Clarendon Avenue toward Victoria Street. Turn right at West 5th Street, left at I-90 Business West, and take the on-ramp to I-90W. Take Exit 9 for US-14W and turn left at US-14W. Turn right at US-14 Alt W (this road may be seasonally closed), and then left at Road 20.

Kane

Kane lies just about ten miles west of Lovell. Established officially in 1912, residents moved in to the area and set up shop many years earlier. Riley Kane, the town's namesake, was a local cowboy from the Mason-Lovell ranch. In the town's prime, it boasted two hotels, two general stores, a pool hall, a dance hall, a school, a railroad depot, and a post office.

In 1965, when the Yellowtail Reservoir was built, many thought the town would be submerged underwater from the dam. The town was condemned; the residents of the dwindling town fought the government, but lost — even though the water never got close to the town.

Established as a mining town for the gold in nearby hills, Kane was more famous for its dance hall. Men and women flocked from surrounding towns on Saturday nights to listen to live music and kick up their heels.

After the decline of the town, rumors started buzzing about buildings being haunted. The old hotel was closed, but the first floor store was still open. One resident recalled going to the store for a soda pop as a child and being too frightened to explore the upstairs because of the ghosts. Apparently, so the story goes, the spirits of jilted cowboys stayed on at the hotel waiting for their lost loves they met at the dance hall.

Today a few tattered buildings exist, but mostly there are just the foundations. A few miles north of the town is where the cemetery is located as well as the famous "Blue Lady." She has been seen walking among the gravestones with a blue haze surrounding her. No one knows who she is or why she frequently appears at the cemetery in Kane.

SIGHTINGS

Big Horn Medicine Wheel

The Big Horn Medicine Wheel is located high up at an elevation of almost 10,000 feet on Medicine Mountain. The wheel is simply made up of local rocks. The central pile of rocks is nearly two feet high and ten feet across. From the center, twenty-eight rock spokes radiate out to the rim, nearly eighty feet from the center. The whole medicine wheel is 245 feet in circumference. The four outer rock piles are aligned with the setting sun and the summer solstice. The twenty-eight spokes are thought to represent the days of the lunar month.

Built around 1300AD, the Big Horn Medicine Wheel is still used for sacred rituals by Native American Indians. Many different legends surround the Big Horn Medicine Wheel. Many versions of how the wheel came to be have been passed down through the years. One such version is that of Burnt Face. Members of the Crow Tribe tell of Burnt Face, who received his name when he fell into a fire as a baby and his face was horribly scarred.

A Native American offering at Bighorn Medicine Wheel. *Courtesy of Bigstock Photos.*

Burnt Face lived a typical childhood among the Indian tribe until he went on his first vision quest. High in the mountains Burnt Face helped save some baby eaglets from a predator. The mother eagle saw this and carried Burnt Face off, smoothing his face along the way. Burnt Face was carried to the top of the Medicine Wheel and dropped off; this is where, after days of fasting, he made the medicine wheel.

The wheel today is used by Indians for ceremonies and many still come to the wheel for vision quests. Visitors to the wheel bring tokens to the spirits that remain; beaded necklaces, colored ribbons, and other sacred objects are placed along the fences.

The Crow Tribe also tell a tale of Chief Red Plume, who hiked to the mountaintop for his vision quest. After he fasted for seven days and nights, spirits started visiting him. The spirits lived on the mountain and took him into the earth. The spirits told him Red Eagle was his protector and gave him a red eagle feather to wear. Years later, while Chief Red Plume was on his deathbed, he told the Crow people that his spirit would always remain at the Medicine Wheel and they could find guidance from him there.

The medicine wheel is not solely used for vision quests; prayers would be made for the sick and atonements were made there for crimes against mother earth. A few tribes also believe the Wheel is a portal to the spirit world. Unfortunately, with the influx of white men making pilgrimages to the Wheel, many modern-day Indians no longer feel comfortable at the Medicine Wheel and have stopped speaking with the spirits at that site.

If you visit the Medicine Mountain, please be respectful of the Native American ways.

Directions To Shoshone Bar and Grill: From Kane, head north on Road 20. Make a slight left to continue on Road 20. Turn left at US-14 Alt W, and make a slight right at East Old Main Street.

Lovell

Covering an area just 1.1 miles long, Lovell is a little gem known for its roses. Dr. William Watts Horsley came to Lovell in the 1920s and noted the climate was perfect for growing roses. Now you can see roses all over the town.

Shoshone Bar and Grill

159 East Old Main Street
Lovell, Wyoming 82431
(307) 548-2099
bighornontap.com

Lovell is a sleepy little town, but is well-known for having one of the most haunted bars in the state. The Shoshone Bar and Grill has more than one mystery surrounding it. Constructed in the early 1940s, the bar was a favorite hangout for Ted Louie, a traveling cigarette and candy salesman. One evening Louie was feeling a little strange and asked the barkeep to help him to a nearby hotel. After the barkeep dropped off Louie, he was never seen again. Apparently, Louie just vanished — he never checked into the hotel and his body was never found. The FBI was brought in to help search for Louie, townspeople were questioned, and rivers, ravines, and prairies were searched, but he was nowhere to be found...that is until his ghost showed up at the Shoshone Bar. Many patrons and employees have felt Louie's presence in the bar. To this day, you can find him usually hanging around the basement or making unearthly sounds.

Other strange occurrences happen at the bar, many of which are attributed to the former owners who still hang around keeping an eye on things and playing pranks. Employees over the years have reported hearing a key unlocking or locking the door to the office. Money has been seen floating through the air and strange electrical phenomena is always a problem. A few patrons and employees have even reported seeing the ghostly apparitions of the former owners and hearing their footsteps and voices.

Directions To Northwest College: Head south on Quebec Avenue toward East Main Street. Turn right at US-310 West, left at US-14 Alt W, and right at South Brent Street. Take the second left onto East 1st Street, turn right at North Absaroka Street, and turn left at West 6th Street.

Powell

A flood irrigation project created the city of Powell. Needing a place to set up camp for the workers, Powell was plotted and eventually grew into a farming community. The natural landscape around the city provides travelers with plenty of water and mountain activities.

Northwest College

231 West 6th Avenue
Powell, Wyoming 82435
(800) 560-4692
www.northwestcollege.edu

Reports started pouring in about strange occurrences in the 1970s. The third seat from the left in the front row of the Nelson Performing Arts auditorium is where the ghost likes to sit. The janitor claims the seat is heavy and nearly impossible to lift back up into place. No mechanical problems are reported with the chair; after it has been lifted up into its position, *something* sits down in the chair. Many of the staff and students believe it's the resident ghost.

Other supernatural events plague the building as well. At night, "shadows" have been seen acting out a play on the stage. On another occasion, during a rehearsal, the performers noticed a large black mass formed over a section of seats near the rear of the auditorium. Cold spots have been felt all over the building and it is not uncommon for objects to move by themselves. Other activity include the lighting system operating by ghostly hands and odd noises heard with no explanation.

In the Green Room, behind the stage, a student, after writing some dirty jokes on a blackboard, was surprised by an apparition. "Adelaide," as the students have named her, was standing behind him wearing a costume described as "like those worn by Eastern European folk dancers with different colors of embroidery on top." She is about 5'5" and had blond shoulder length hair. Adelaide has been seen often in the theater area; occasionally a student will take a seat in her chair and tell her his problems. She has a presence in the building, but is not the only presence that sticks around.

One teacher had enough of the spirit's shenanigans and decided to confront "it." The next day, his office, which was located in the makeup room, was in shambles — books, papers, and generally anything not nailed down were strewn about.

The auditorium is only one of the buildings haunted at the college. Ashley Hall also has reports of strange occurrences. Residents have reported unearthly footsteps walking down the halls, chairs and tables scraping against the floor, or cabinet doors opening and slamming shut. Stoves in the building have a habit of turning on full blast by themselves, burners and all. Summer cleaning crews have scratched their heads when steaming buckets of water turn ice cold and then back to hot within minutes.

Directions To Heart Mountain: From Northwest College, head west on West 6th Street. Turn left onto North Cheyenne Street, right at US-14 Alt W, and right at Road 19. Continue straight onto Lane 13H and turn right at Road 19.

Heart Mountain

Powell, Wyoming 82435
(307) 764-2320
www.heartmountain.us

America was changed forever on December 7, 1941, for it was on that fateful day that Japan successfully executed a sneak attack on Pearl Harbor. From that day forward Americans were not-so-welcoming towards Japanese Americans. All over the country Japanese were sent to internment camps, and Heart Mountain was one of those camps.

Opening August 12, 1942, the Heart Mountain Relocation Center welcomed Japanese Americans, soon housing nearly 11,000 people. The people who were sent to these camps left everything they had behind: their jobs, property, and almost all of their possessions except for what they could carry. Life was not as pleasant as one would hope. Barbed wire and guard towers kept the people in and the wild cowboys, whose sentiment was at the very least hostile, out. Whole families lived in unfurnished one-room barracks with a communal bathroom. The barracks were primitive, with only tar paper to keep them from the harsh Wyoming elements.

Over time, the residents of Heart Mountain created a democratic self-government and a newspaper. A few of the local farmers welcomed the internees to help harvest their crops and with farm needs. Despite the low quality health care inside the camp, nearly 550 babies were born in the camp.

For the most part the Japanese Americans held their heads high as American citizens and, in 1943, thirty-eight young internees volunteered for the Army. The United States reinstated the draft for many interned and thousands volunteered to serve, even though they were unjustly yanked from their lives and held captive in barbed wire camps. Many within the barb wire in Heart Mountain fought for the United States in Italy and the Pacific. Still others resisted the draft and were sentenced to federal prison.

The U.S. War Department announced the revocation of the West Coast Exclusion order against Japanese Americans on December 17, 1944. The last of the Heart Mountain Japanese Americans left in the fall of 1945 to start their lives over.

Many of the camp's buildings were auctioned off, and today just a few buildings remain where thousands once lived and thrived. Many visitors to the Heart Mountain Relocation Center feel as though they are being followed as they wander the property. During the night, when all is quiet, you can hear mysterious footsteps and see shadows darting around the remaining buildings. These shadow people are common to Heart Mountain and visitors to the complex have been talking about them for years.

Directions To Irma Hotel: From Heart Mountain, head south on Road 19. Turn left at Lane 13H, continue onto Road 19, turn right at US-14 Alt W, and turn right again at US-14 W. *(You will see signs for Yellowstone; the destination will be on the left.)*

Cody

Located directly west of Cody, Cedar Mountain has two peaks, which are separated by the Shoshone River. Just west of Cedar "Spirit" Mountain is the Buffalo Bill Reservoir and State Park. The dam that holds the reservoir was the tallest in the world at its completion in 1910. Located in Cedar Mountain is a massive cavern system called the Spirit Mountain Cave. Once a national monument, the cave has since been closed due to its remoteness and difficulty in reaching the site.

Discovered in 1908 by bobcat hunter, Ned Frost, you can still explore the cave by securing a permit from the BLM. The cave is extensive and is thought to go all the way to the Shoneshone River. Much of the cave has remained untouched and unexplored. During the construction for the Shonshone Canyon Conduit through the Cedar Mountain, several caverns were discovered containing hydrogen sulfide gas, which can be fatal.

Many hikers have reported strange supernatural events on the mountain and in the cave. There have been rumors the cave is home to a race of little people. The local Indians believed the steam that used to rise from the mountain, when natural geysers were still active within the mountain, was the mountain's spirit escaping. Today hikers report hearing phantom footsteps following them up the mountain and through the cave system. When the footsteps get close, the hikers always turn to look and there is never anyone behind them. Are these footsteps from hikers who lost their lives in the caves or are they the little people thought to inhabit the mountain.

Buffalo Bill Cody may have been buried on Lookout Mountain, near Golden, Colorado, but his final wishes were to be buried on Cedar Mountain overlooking his namesake town Cody. Buffalo Bill Cody died in 1917 while visiting his sister in Denver. According to his wife and close friends, his final wishes were to be buried on Lookout Mountain. The citizens of Wyoming were outraged and claimed that he had stated several times that he wanted to be buried on Cedar Mountain. His 1906 will describes his wishes to be buried on the mountain overlooking Cody, with a massive red stone buffalo marking his gravesite. By the time of his death, a new will had been put into place leaving his wife full control of his burial plans. It will never be known which mountain he wanted to be buried on. Today Buffalo Bill Cody's grave is covered with a thick slab of concrete after several citizens of Cody tried to steal his body from Colorado to bury him in Wyoming.

Many Wyoming residents believe Buffalo Bill is actually buried on Cedar Mountain. During the time Bill's body was prepared and during the several months wait to be buried, it is thought that men from Cody switched the body with another man who resembled Buffalo Bill. This could be plausible since decomposition would have taken place and the body would have been difficult to recognize. After the switch, Buffalo Bill's body was brought to Cedar Mountain and buried there, as the citizens thought he wanted.

However, there is only one official grave on Cedar Mountain — Breck Moran (1907-1954). An important figure in Cody's development, Moran ran the Cody newspaper and in the 1940s was one of the founders of the KODI radio station that still broadcasts today. Also, a marker has been placed where the famous Ebb Tarr ashes were spread on the mountain. Ebb was a Buffalo Bill impersonator who died in 2007.

SIGHTINGS

The Skeleton

Before there were horses, a group of young Arapahos set out one crisp autumn to search for game. While crossing a shallow creek one of the young warriors felt a sharp pain in his ankle. As the group walked on, the ankle swelled and the pain grew unbearable. Setting up camp for the night, the warrior hoped that a good night's sleep would cure his ankle for the rest of the journey.

When the warrior woke the next morning, his ankle had swelled so badly that he could not continue his journey with his group. The rest of the group decided to leave him. Cutting willows and tall grass to make him a shelter, the group continued. They told him to return to the village once his ankle got better rather than trying to catch up with the group.

Several days passed with no improvement to his ankle. Nearly out of food, he was starting to worry about his future — and then it got worse. Snow fell one night imprisoning him in his shelter. A few more days passed and he noticed a small heard of buffalo rooting through the snow close to his shelter. He grabbed his bow and shot the fattest one he could see. It fell dead. The warrior then crawled out of his shelter to the buffalo. Skinning it and dragging the meat into his shelter. He prepared his fire and threw a rib section on to cook.

As night fell, the ribs were ready to eat, but just as he reached for a section of meat he heard crunching footfalls in the snow. Nervous as to who the intruder might be, he grabbed his knife, bow, and arrows. Moments later the flap opened revealing a skeleton garbed in a robe peering down at the lame warrior. Frightened the warrior looked away. "You must not be frightened of me," exclaimed the skeleton. "I have taken pity on you. Now you must take pity on me. Give me a piece of those roast ribs to eat, for I am very hungry." The young warrior reached out, grabbed a large piece of rib meat, and offered it to the skeleton. Surprisingly the skeleton chewed the piece of meat and swallowed it.

"It was I who gave you the pain in your ankle," said the skeleton. "It was I who caused your ankle to swell so that you could not continue on the hunt. If you had gone on with your companions, you would have been killed. The day they left you here, an enemy war party made a charge upon them, and they were all killed. I am the one who saved your life."

Then the bony fingers of the skeleton reached out and touched the warriors ankle — immediately the swelling and pain disappeared. The skeleton explained further that enemies are close by, but if he followed the skeleton he would be led to safety back at his village.

The next morning, the skeleton and warrior walked through the woods and over high hills until the skeleton led the warrior up onto a steep ridge. At the summit the skeleton disappeared, but, as the warrior looked down, he could see the teepees of his people.

Irma Hotel

1192 Sheridan Avenue
Cody, Wyoming 82414
(307) 587-4221
www.irmahotel.com

Buffalo Bill Cody built the Irma Hotel in 1902, calling it "just the sweetest hotel that ever was." Bill had two suites and an office he used in the hotel. The town of Cody is his namesake and the Irma Hotel was named for his daughter. Inviting all his friends to the hotel, including Annie Oakley, Calamity Jane, and Frederick Remington, Bill held court at his favorite place. Holding tryouts for his Wild West show in several

Annie Oakley. *Courtesy of Library of Congress.*

Buffalo Bill Cody hosted royalty at the Irma Hotel... Here he is with the Prince of Monaco. *Courtesy of Library of Congress.*

empty lots next to the hotel, Bill invited them back to the bar for a drink. Bill had many visitors at the hotel as well, including European royalty and friends from exotic places all over the world.

The building was constructed out of river rock quarried out of local sandstone and the river rock from the Beck Lake south of town. The fireplace is constructed from rock, ore, and fossils from the Big Horn basin. The most famous and most photographed in all of Cody is the bar. Made of cherry wood, it is original to the hotel.

Today the hotel has been completely renovated with modern bathrooms and air-conditioning. In 1929, an addition was added to the northwest side and, in 1977, another addition was constructed on the southwest side. Buffalo Bill's private suites are available to guests and you can even sidle up to the bar where Bill and his friends drank.

Most of the ghost stories come from the original part of the hotel. Room 16 is Irma's room — employees at the hotel have seen the rocking chair in Irma's room quietly swaying back and forth. In Room 35, guests sometimes see a Confederate soldier; he is usually pacing or looking out the window as if waiting for something.

Many employees also claim that Buffalo Bill Cody is still there keeping watch over his beloved hotel. Guests claim to hear boots with spurs walking down the halls late at night.

One employee claims that each morning while setting up the dining room she would hear her name called out. When she would look around, she would be alone...or was she? A flight attendant came downstairs one morning clad in her underwear claiming that a spirit had sexually assaulted her the previous night. It is well-known that Bill liked women, and the employees all agreed it must have been Bill. The flight attendant told the story to her friends and that room became quite popular among flight attendants. If they had an encounter, they were quiet about it, as only one story surfaced of a ghostly sexual assault.

One spirited tale comes from the cook of the hotel. Once while in the basement alone he heard a conversation. Describing it as "Old West" cowboy talk, it spooked the cook enough for him not to ever return alone to the basement.

Speaking of hearing ghosts at the Irma, one guest had a restless night after listening to a wild game of poker being played on the floor above her. After inquiring about it the next morning, the manager on-duty claimed no one was playing poker and that she was on the top floor. He explained the spirits must have been out that night.

Other sightings within the Irma include a Civil War solider seen in the dining area and near the old cherry wood bar. Irma herself has been seen wandering the halls and a woman known as the "Lady in White" has been seen roaming the hallways of the second floor where occasionally guests have encountered her in their rooms. The kitchen is an area where an aggressive spirit likes to hang out, perhaps the original cook, still trying to prepare dinners.

Directions To Cowboy Bar: From Irma Hotel, head east on Sheridan Avenue toward 12th Street. Continue onto US-14 East and turn right at WY-120E.

Meeteetse

Meeteetse means 'meeting place' in Shoshone, and that is just what the town was to many, especially the cowboys at the Pitchfork Ranch, which was started in 1879. It is notable for being the first cattle ranching operation in the Big Horn Basin. Besides being one of the largest cattle ranches around, the Pitchfork Ranch is known for having the last colony of the endangered Black Footed Ferret.

The town had a reputation for being wild and, in 1906, seven saloons, one store, two banks, and two hotels within the city's limits cemented the town's wild ways for years to come. Today, the town looks much as it did one hundred years ago: wooden boardwalks, watering troughs, and hitching rails still stand as if you have stepped back in time. The only difference is today the town of Meeteetse has more churches than bars.

The Cowboy Bar

1936 State Street
Meeteetse, Wyoming 82433
(307) 868-2585

The Cowboy Bar was constructed in 1893. As the bar stands today, it has a total of fifty-six bullet holes and one shotgun blast in its walls and ceiling. The famous outlaw Butch Cassidy resided in Meeteetse and even signed a petition for a new bridge in 1886. A frequent patron to The Cowboy Bar, he was arrested in front of the establishment in 1894.

Reports of footsteps frequent the bar as well as reports of steak orders from disembodied voices. Occasionally full glasses of beer fall off the bar and land on the floor without spilling a drop. Strange occurrences for sure. The atmosphere is well worth the price of a drink...just to see if it slips by you and ends up on the floor.

Directions To Hot Springs County Library: From Cowboy Bar, head southeast on WY-120E. Turn left at North 6th Street and then take the first right onto Arapahoe Street.

Butch Cassidy frequented The Cowboy Bar.
Courtesy of Library of Congress.

Thermopolis

Hot springs are the draw to Thermopolis. Open to the public since 1896, the city claims its hot springs are the largest in the world.

Hot Springs County Library

344 Arapahoe Street
Thermopolis, WY 82443
(307) 864-3104
www.wsl.state.wy.us

Many citizens have heard rumors about their library being haunted and even more may have experienced something strange in the building. The night janitors only last a few months before quitting their jobs and employees never stay late by themselves. What could be spooking all these people? According to rumors, shadowy figures dart between the stacks and unexplained noises are heard all over the library. Each morning when the librarian opens up, books are strewn across the floors and tables. Disturbances seem to be more common in the early evening and night at the Hot Springs County Library; you should be safe going during the day to check out your favorite book.

Directions To Hot Springs County Museum and Cultural Center: From Hot Springs County Library, head west on Arapahoe Street toward North 4th Street. Take the second left onto North 5th Street and then the first right onto Broadway Street.

Hot Springs County Museum and Cultural Center

700 Broadway
Thermopolis, Wyoming 82443
(307) 864-5183
www.hschistory.org

The Hot Springs County Museum and Cultural Center is more of a compound comprised of the main museum building, a schoolhouse, a 'poverty flats' house, a caboose, and an agricultural building. Inside the museum, Old West artifacts litter the building. Indian objects, Old West relics, and local 'stuffed' wildlife all set a scene for what life was like over one hundred years ago. A Thermopolis Main Street Exhibit showcases some of the stores that made the town what it is today. Most of the objects within these exhibits are from the actual store, which sat on the Main Street of Thermopolis.

The building that houses the museum has been around for nearly one hundred years, originally opening as the Ford Garage. A few years later, in the 1930s, the building housed a Coca Cola Plant with a bowling alley in the basement. The next business to move in was the Technical College of the Rockies and finally in the late 1970s the museum took over the building.

With all this history packed into the building, it is not wonder that a few spirits can't help but hang around. Docents and patrons at the museum report hearing loud footsteps walking down deserted hallways and sometimes even following them. There are also reports late at night of glowing orbs floating around inside the museum and outside near the museum buildings. Visitors are often startled when they see a woman sitting in one of the display chairs wearing nineteenth century clothing — and then suddenly fade away. Others still claim to have seen a woman wearing Victorian clothing walking around the theater area when no shows are going on.

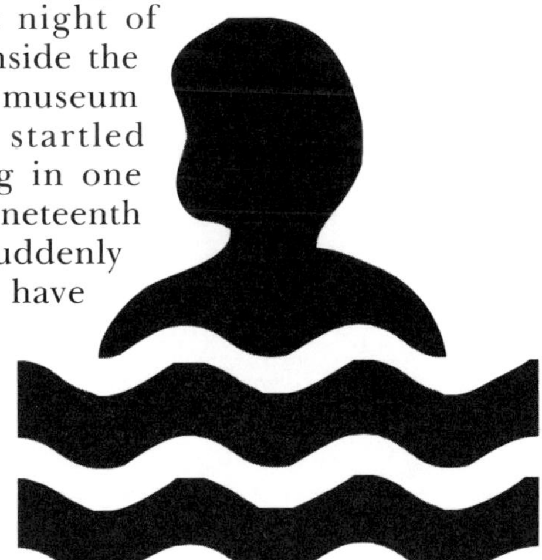

Is the spirit that haunts the Hot Springs County Museum the former tenant of the 'poverty flats' house? The woman who owned it was said to be an eccentric recluse who read palms and told fortunes for money. Some locals say she was frighteningly accurate. Perhaps Mrs. Hemming was unhappy with her home being moved or maybe it's another spirit attached to an object in the museum or with the building.

SIGHTINGS

Crop Circles

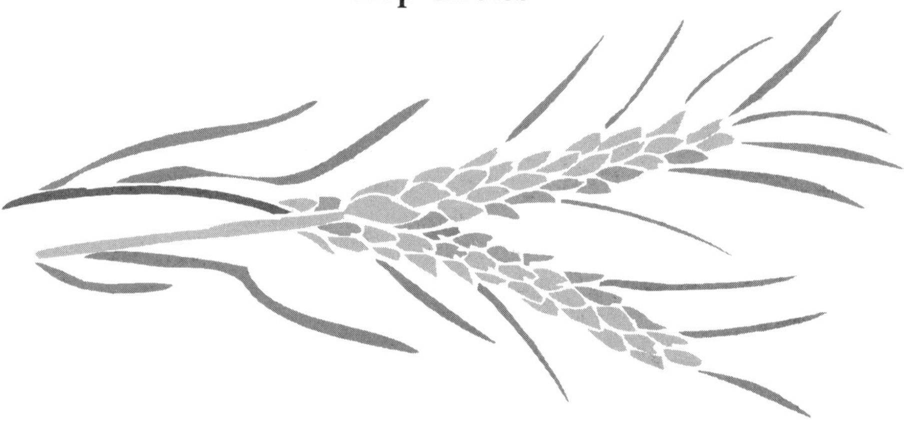

In 1678, the first crop circle was reported in Hartfordshire, England. A woodcut with a picture of a devil wheeling a scythe tells of a farmer who refuses to pay a mower a reasonable rate for reaping his oats. The farmer swore he would rather have the devil do it. The following morning the farmer woke up to his crop being harvested, but in rounded circles, with an exactness that would be impossible for a human to do, especially in the pitch black of night. The farmer was so terrified by what he found... he refused to enter the circle to collect his harvest.

Crop circles started showing up in the United States in the 1920s, but has had an increase in frequency since the 1960s with at least 190 new formations documented in 1999.

On November 15, 1966, two hunters were out looking for elk when they noticed strange lights dancing on the next ridge. The next day, they made their way over to the ridge — and discovered a semi-circular area pressed flat. A fawn was found at the perimeter of the circle with its head severed clean off. No sign of blood or other abrasions were found on or near the deer.

TRIP 4

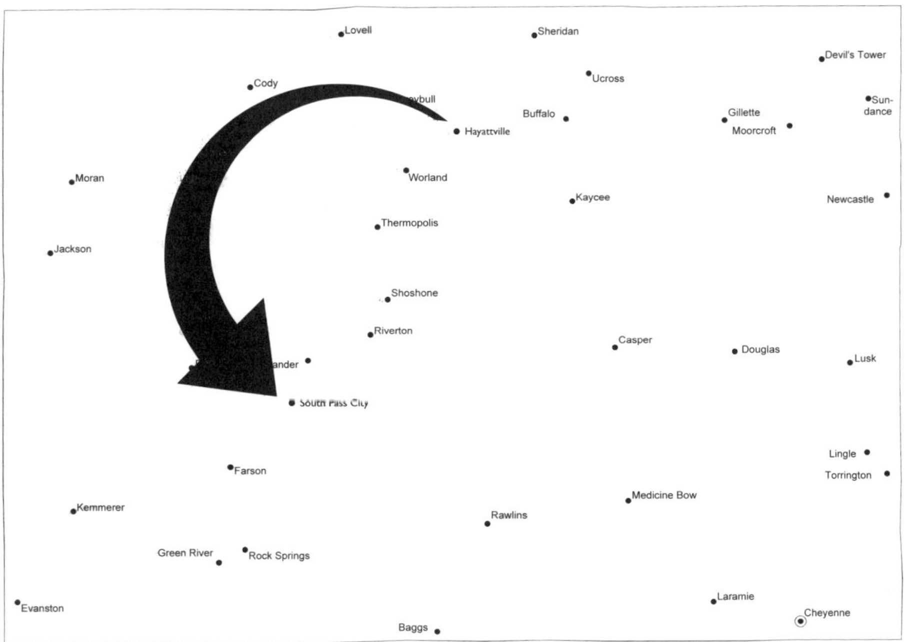

HAYATTVILLE TO SOUTH PASS CITY

HAYATTVILLE

Hyattville has the cozy population of seventy-three people. The town is named after Samuel Hyatt, a shop owner. Today the town serves as a gateway to the Medicine Lodge State Park.

MEDICINE LODGE STATE PARK

The creek at the Medicine Lodge State Park is believed to contain supernatural powers to protect and heal. The Shoshone Indians visited the creek often. Before war, the Indians would bathe in the waters for protection and endurance. Babies were dipped in the waters to ensure a long life, and sick Shoshone Indians traveled to the creek for relief of their ailments.

The creek that runs through the State Park is not the primary attraction, though. The pictographs and petroglyphs are also sacred, but viewed by tourists as Indian graffiti. This could not be further from the truth. Indians believe the rock is a living thing and drawing and carving into the rock is a "spiritual union" with the rock. These symbols at Medicine Lodge are sacred to the Indians and make this place even more sacred not just because of the water, but because of the union with the rock.

Art collectors who remove pieces of the rock to display in galleries, homes, and museums are destroying the bond and defacing the sacred spot for Indians past, present, and future.

The Medicine Creek Lodge offers visitors camping, corrals, a picnic area, fishing, playgrounds, and trails. The site is open year round, but the Visitor's Center is only open May-September.

DIRECTIONS TO GEBO: From Cold Springs Road, turn left at Aikaiai Road and right at WY-31W, continuing straight onto North Sherman Avenue. Turn left at US-16E, right at US-20E, right at Sand Draw Road, and then left at Gebo.

Gebo

Like many ghost towns in the west, Gebo was founded on the sweat, tears, and dreams of the coal miners. Springing up in 1906, the town was named after Samuel Gebo, a coal mine developer in the area.

Gebo was once a thriving town, with nearly 1,200 people living within the town's limits; six hundred of the residents worked in the local coal mine. Such promise arose from mining in Gebo that people flocked to the town to open up pool halls, schools, banks, boarding houses, and of course brothels. Unfortunately, by 1932, money had run out of the mine and the residents soon moved on to another promising town. In 1938, the coal mines in Gebo officially closed.

Samuel Gebo invested in several bad mines, one of which was located in Canada. The local Indians called the mountain the mine was located in 'Mountain that Walks', due to the earthquakes that plagued the mountain daily. On April 29, 1903, a large earthquake struck the town of Frank, killing seventy-six people, possibly more. The miners had enough and walked away from the town and Samuel Gebo's mine.

On July 10, 1940, the day that Samuel stuck his head in his oven and killed himself, many thought the Frank Mine was the start of his undoing. Samuels's wife drowned just five months later.

What remained in the ghost town decayed over the years and, finally in 1971, the Federal Bureau of Land Management bulldozed the town. Today only a few structures and the cemetery remain. Through the years, many family members moved the remains of their loved ones to larger cemeteries, but a few of the graves remain; mainly infants that barely survived a day or week, but also some adults remain — a reminder of how hard life was in the mining town.

As you stroll the ground that was once Gebo, you may notice the dugouts — rocks with trash piles near them — where the poor lived. Old timbers still stand at the mine openings and a few buildings stand, which are sagging and weather worn. Can you hear the voices of the past blow by your ears in the wind? Paranormal hunters who visited the town site say you can. Visitors to the area report feeling watched and followed. Some have heard babies crying near the cemetery and voices echoing down the empty streets of a time gone by.

Directions To Acme Theater: From Gebo, head east on Old Gebo Road toward Sand Draw Road. Continue onto Sand Draw Road and turn right onto US-20E. Continue straight onto North 6th Street (North 6th Street turns slightly right and becomes US-20E) and then turn right at US-26 W/E Main Street.

Riverton

Created during the great Land Rush, Riverton was one of the only places where squatters could legally acquire the town land they were living on. Farmers on the outskirts of town were subject to a lottery to acquire the free land they desired.

In 1914, Wyoming Tie & Tiber Company received a contract with the Chicago & Northwestern Railroad for railroad ties. This created plenty of work that has never ceased in the town.

Acme Theater

312 East Main Street
Riverton, Wyoming 82501
(307) 856-3415
www.gabeltheatres.com

Built in 1920 by Belle Monte, an influential businesswoman of Riverton, Acme Theater stands virtually untouched by time. Tom Knight bought the theater in the 1950s and today the Gabel Theater Company runs the movie house. The theater is still only one screen and plays movies twice Sunday through Thursdays and three times on Fridays and Saturdays.

Over the years, moviegoers have witnessed a ghostly vaudeville performer standing in the balcony during late night shows at the theater. He only shows himself on occasion, perhaps when he feels no one is looking. Many people claim they feel his presence rather than see him, but you may just be the lucky one who spies the vaudeville ghost.

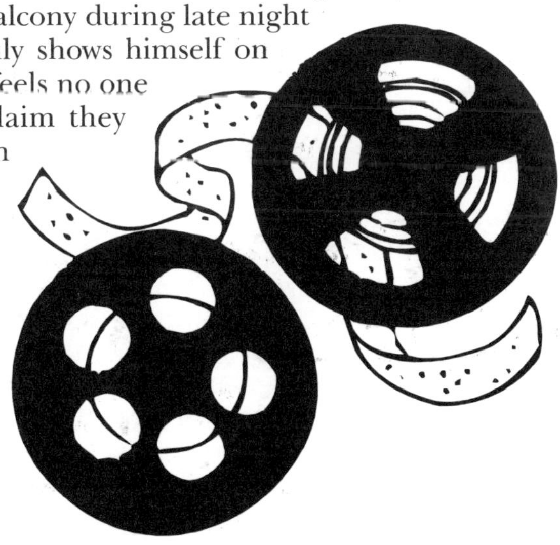

Directions To The Old Broker Restaurant: From Acme Theater, head west on East Main Street toward North 3rd Street. Make a U-turn at South 2nd Street.

Old Broker Restaurant

203 East Main Street
Riverton Wyoming 82501
(307) 856-0555

Old Broker Restaurant in Riverton is said to be haunted by a little girl. The spirit once walked right by the former owner of the restaurant... only to disappear seconds later. A former employee describes her as being around seven years old, blond, shoulder length hair, and wearing a white shirt. She is very friendly and likes to greet employees and patrons of the restaurant with a cute little 'Hello' while they are enjoying their meal. Employees and diners describe the restaurant as being creepy and always feeling as if you are being watched. On several occasions, the doorknobs rattle when no one is near and the lights have been known to flicker for unknown reasons.

Directions To Saint Stephens Indian Mission: From Old Broker Restaurant, head east on East Main Street toward South 3rd Street and turn right at WY-789S. Turn right onto Rendezvous Road, left onto Mission Road, and left onto St. Stephens Road.

Saint Stephens Indian Mission

St. Stephens, Wyoming 82524
www.ssimf.com

Father John Jutz came out west from Buffalo, New York, to establish a school on the Wind River Indian Reservation. Out of a tent, Father Jutz started the first services and school. Later Bishop O'Conner from Omaha, Nebraska, joined Father Jutz and built a more suitable building with four rooms. Soon Father Jutz was called back east and was replaced by Father Ponziglione. It was not long before more buildings were built with a convent in 1887, which was still being used by the Franciscan nuns until 2003 when the building was demolished for safety reasons. Through the years the school thrived, housing Indian children during the week. On Sundays, the children returned home.

The first setback was in 1928, when a fire destroyed many of the buildings including the church and boy's dormitory. The buildings were rebuilt, but, in 1939, with the acquisition of buses, children were no longer housed at the school. In the mid-1950s a gym was built as well as a high school building. Only open for ten years, the high school was shut down due to lack of funding. Only a few buildings remain, but the spirits of the children who learned and thrived at the school remain.

The Keil Gym seems to be the center of the paranormal activity at the school. Sounds of balls are heard even when no balls are loose in the gym. Basketball was a favorite activity among the students at Saint Stephens. Children have been seen in the gym and around the grounds of Saint Stephens as well, usually out of the corner of a visitor's eye, but, when they take a second look, the figure is gone. Some of the sisters at St. Stephens have claimed they see apparitions of departed nuns gliding along — they are reported to have no faces or feet visible. Other activity in the gym are balls of light that dance around the empty building at night illuminating the inside.

Directions To Blue Sky Hall: From Saint Stephens Indian Mission, head northwest and turn right at WY-789N. Turn left at Rendezvous Road, a slight right at WY-137, and then left at Plunket Road/Ethete Road.

Ethete

Not much is known about the city of Ethete other than it is located in Freemont County, in the Riverton metro area, and has a population of 1,455 residents.

Blue Sky Hall

506 Ethete Road
Ethete, Wyoming 82520

Within the Blue Sky Hall's walls resides a spirit that likes to rearrange items and occasionally throw objects around the hall. A few visitors to the building have encountered an apparition, gliding gently through the rooms and down the hallways. Disembodied voices and screams also echo throughout the building, but especially in the back rooms. Voices are heard coming from the fitness area too. Locals claim the voices are of departed spirits left behind from when funeral services were held at the hall. Today the tribal committee is housed there.

Directions To Fort Washakie: From Blue Sky Hall, head south on Ethete Road/ Plunket Road. Turn right at US-287N and then left at Black Coal Drive. Continue on North Fork Road and turn right at Washakie Street (You'll need to make a left to stay on Washakie Street) and then take the first left onto 1st Street.

Fort Washakie

In 1878, after negotiation by Chief Washakie with Sacagawea as his interpreter, Fort Brown officially changed its name. Besides being the burial ground for Sacagawea, her family, and Chief Washakie, the fort now stands as the home to the Shoshone Tribal Cultural Center. Today many of the original buildings from the fort still stand in the historic district.

In several areas of the reservation and within the original fort you can hear a long-ago Powwow commencing. Some even say you can hear the crackle of a fire and feel vibrations under your feet.

Other reports that often reoccur are of being followed at night by a small black spirit. Occasionally reports relay the spirit will whisper your name or play other tricks on you by tipping your hat while it is on your head or tugging on your clothing.

At the Fort Washakie School, the spirit of a little girl is said to remain, entertaining herself by your actions. She is said to giggle often and is only interrupted by another spirit, which is known to sneeze and cough. These disembodied voices come from rumors that the school was built on an unmarked grave and even more rumors

The spirit of a little girl coughs and giggles near the school at Fort Washakie.
Courtesy of Library of Congress.

Is Sacagawea buried at the Shoshone Cemetery? Some say no.
Courtesy of Library of Congress.

circulate that a student died in the basement. I could not authenticate either the grave or the death of the student, but nonetheless spirits still hang around the schoolhouse.

I cannot mention Fort Washakie without bringing up Sacagawea. There are no reported sightings of her spirit or anything supernatural about her or her grave, but she does have a mysterious ending to her adventurous life.

Near Fort Washakie, Sacagawea is buried; you can still see her grave along with her nephew's grave and a memorial to her son Baptiste. She had returned to her Shoshone people in Fort Washakie before her death and was buried on April 9, 1884. Sacagawea was the translator for Chief Washakie while he was in negotiations for reservation land. She was often seen wearing peace medals given to her by Lewis and Clark. She is buried in the Sacagawea Cemetery near the foothills of the Wind River Mountains.

According to government records, Sacagawea died many years earlier on December 12, 1812, at Fort Lia in North Dakota, of fever. It was only until a book came out in the early 1900s that claimed a female Indian guide who traveled with Lewis and Clark died in 1884 at the age of one hundred in Wyoming. The book was written from stories of the elders of the Shoshones; many believe the Wyoming gravesite is the final resting place for Sacagawea...or is it?

Directions To South Pass City: From Fort Washakie, head northeast on 1st Street. Take the first right to stay onto Washakie Street and then turn left at North Fork Road. Continue straight onto Black Coal Drive and turn right at US-287S. Continue onto WY-28W and turn left at South Pass City Road, left at S Street, and another left at South Pass Main Street. *(Note: Only open May 15-September 30, 9 a.m. to 6 p.m. daily.)*

South Pass City

125 Main Street
South Pass City, Wyoming 82520
(307) 332-3684
www.southpasscity.com

A trapper discovered gold in the hills of South Pass City in 1842. According to the *Sweetwater Miner* dated March 24, 1869, the trapper was killed by Indians before he could lay claim to the gold he found. It was not until 1867 when the Clarissa Gold Mine was founded that miners flocked to the area in search of their fortune. Several towns in the area formed overnight; most have since faded back into the countryside, but South Pass City is the best preserved town in all of Wyoming.

Like most mining towns in the west, South Pass had plenty of trouble with outlaws and unsavory characters. Saloons were plentiful and so were the girls trying to make a buck anyway they could. Calamity Jane stayed in South Pass for a while and Buffalo Bill Cody worked for the Pony Express.

Is Polly roaming the streets of South Pass City looking for her next victim? *Courtesy of Library of Congress.*

The drunken gunfights and outlaws were not the only problem the townspeople had to watch for. On several occasions the local Indians would attack the town, once burning down a portion of it. In 1867, the Sioux Indians attacked the miners who worked the Clarissa Mine; the miners fled in fear, but returned the next year. The Indians continued to attack the mine; stealing horses, mules, supplies, and even killing several miners.

The town only lasted a few years. By 1875, less than one hundred people remained in the town. The Clarissa Mine had run out of gold and the Indians were relentless, even with the nearby Fort Stambaugh protecting the miners.

One resident who never left, though, is Polly Bartlett, who, along with her father, operated a small inn near South Pass. Offering travelers a hot meal and warm bed, it seemed like a great place to stop and rest before heading into town. It was a great place for Polly who would prepare the travelers' dinner with a special ingredient...arsenic. Once the travelers had their meal, she would rob them of their gold. Rumor has it that Polly and her father became quite wealthy helping their guests get a good meal and some rest. The tale ends when a vengeful relative of one of Polly's victims showed up and took the law into her own hands. Polly died from a shotgun blast; she is buried in an unmarked grave near the edge of town.

Polly's spirit has been seen wandering the streets of South Pass, quietly walking down the dirt roads and even entering some buildings. Next time you are wandering those same streets look twice at the costumed employee...it might just be Polly wanting to offer you a meal and a cozy bed.

Trip 5

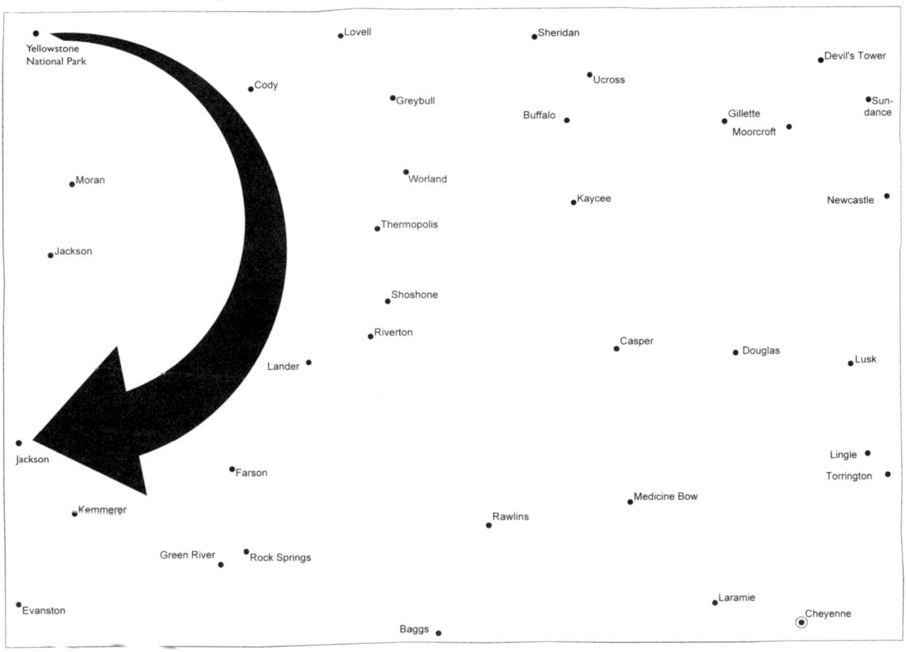

Yellowstone National Park to Jackson

Yellowstone National Park

Note: When you enter Yellowstone, you will receive a map and information material about the park. Please follow the map to the different locations listed.

Yellowstone is filled with the spirits of visitors and workers who have met an unfortunate end, not to mention those who died of natural causes and loved the park so much they came back in death.

Filled with unsurpassed beauty and overwhelming adventure, Yellowstone National Park is full of dangers. Bison, bears, wolves, and other dangerous animals are abundant. Geysers and hot pools of water hold a deathly curiosity to pets, children, and adults alike. Loose rocks, lightning, fire, poisonous plants, and extreme weather are all killers at the park.

The park itself is located on a volcano — not a regular volcano, but one of only a few super volcanoes around the world. The massive caldera crater is nearly 1,500 miles, compared to Mount St. Helens crater, which is only two square miles. When Mount St. Helens erupted in 1980, it blew 80,000 feet in the air in fifteen minutes and spread over twenty-two miles a whopping 1.4 billion thousand cubic yards of ash, which killed

Many visitors died from Yellowstone's dangers before fences were erected; photo circa 1903. *Courtesy of Library of Congress.*

Hidden dangers are everywhere at Yellowstone. *Courtesy of Bigstock Photos*

fifty-seven people. One could only imagine what the super volcano under Yellowstone could do. Predictions speculate the ash from the Yellowstone volcano would cover the Pacific Coast and encompass the Midwest. The eruption would change weather patterns and kill millions.

Some of the earliest deaths in the park can be attributed to Indians, cold, and snow, including avalanches. In the lawless days of the Wild West, problems were solved by the end of a gun; this took care of more than a few early souls within the park. There also have been too many men and women who just walked away and disappeared for the park not to be haunted.

Vanished

LeRoy R. Piper is one such man who stepped out of the Fountain Hotel one clear night and was never seen again. It was a pleasant July 30th night in 1900, and he had just finished dinner and had purchased a cigar. Piper was a bank cashier on his way to San Francisco from Ohio to settle his uncle's estate. Piper was wearing dinner attire: a blue suit, a white monogrammed shirt, black lace patent leather shoes, and a derby hat; he was not in the habit of exploring the wilderness, especially in that attire. What happened to LeRoy Piper as he stepped onto the porch

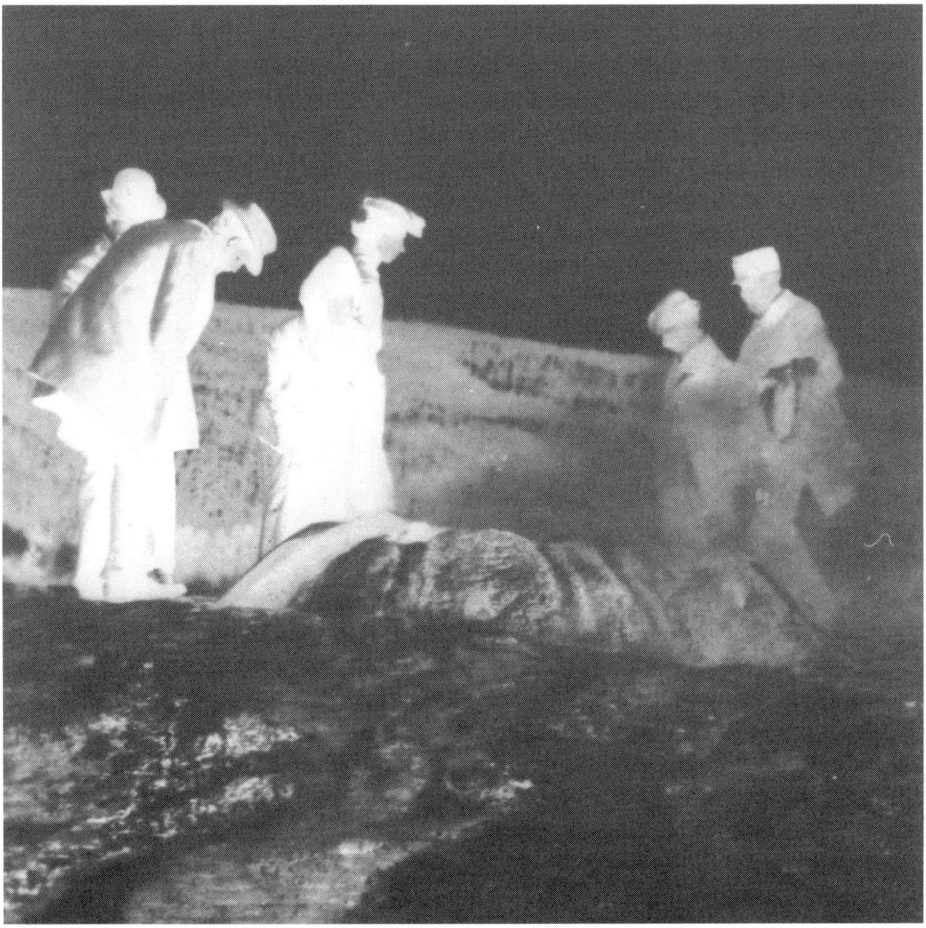

no one will ever know. Did he wander too close to a geyser and fall into one of the hot springs? Perhaps a bear or another animal snatched him up? Piper is one of the many missing person cases in Yellowstone that is unsolved.

On July 12, 1966 a young boy of eight wandered away from his family at the Cascade picnic area, never to been seen again. The National Park Service searched for three weeks by ground, air, and with dogs; he was never found. His parents hired a psychic to find the boy, but she was unable to identify his whereabouts.

Like Piper's, the boy's remains were never found. Did they step off into another dimension? Were they consumed by animals, or fall into a scalding pit of water? The park may never reveal its secrets, but if you look closely, it will let you glance into its surreptitious past.

Nez Perce Picnic Area

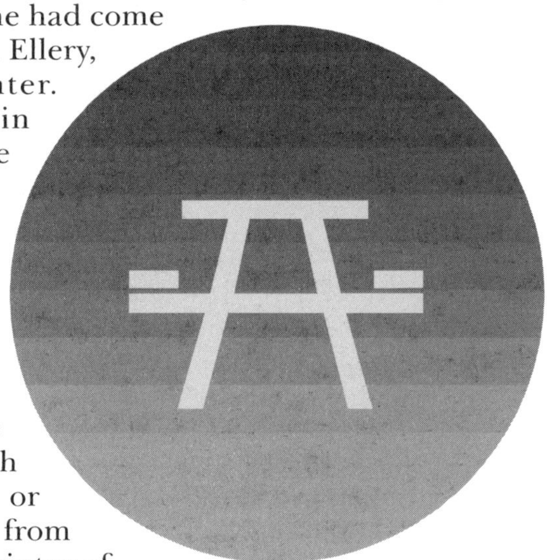

Near the Nez Perce Picnic area overlooking the Firehole River is the lonely grave of Mattie. She had come to the park with her husband, Ellery, and their newborn daughter. They settled into life within the confines of Yellowstone nicely, living seasonally at the Firehole Hotel just off the banks of the pristine Firehole River. Mattie had a secret...she was dying. Tuberculosis was contracted easily in the late nineteenth century. Mattie could have contracted it in her youth working in the Textile Mills or by her first husband who died from the mysterious disease. The winter of 1889 was hard for Mattie and her husband as the couple stayed on at the hotel through the winter as caretakers. On March 2, 1889, Mattie succumbed to the disease. Ellery knew of the love she had for the park and buried her near the hotel overlooking the river.

That April, Ellery moved away to better care for his now one-year-old daughter, but it was not long before he returned to the park to be close to his wife, leaving his daughter in the care of Mattie's sister in Washington State.

In 1891, the Firehole Hotel burned down; visitors were redirected to the new grander Fountain Hotel a few miles away. Ellery was saddened by the loss of the hotel he shared with his wife, but never faltered in visiting his Mattie. Tragedy struck Ellery once again when his daughter died at the tender age of nineteen. Ellery kept on at the park for a mere three years more when his heath dictated he move to a warmer climate — and away from Mattie. On April 17, 1922, Ellery died; his wishes were to be buried next to his wife above the Firehole River. Times had changed, though, and the National Park Service refused his final wish. Instead, Ellery was buried in Los Angeles away from his beloved wife.

Visitors who stumble upon the grave are drawn to it mysteriously. Quietly returning each time they visit the park, some leave flowers while others just offer company. Mattie has been seen walking quietly along the banks of the river or just sitting beside her grave, humming a tune.

Miss Victoria Vendables

Stories of ghostly hitchhikers frighten motorists across the country, and Yellowstone is not immune to this type of ghost. Driving through the historic park, you certainly have plenty to watch for: animals in the road, navigating curves, and of course other traffic you may come upon. However, you would never think you might come across a lonely spirit looking for a ride. That is exactly what happened to one man as he set out across the park during a heavy downpour.

Todd was driving from the north entrance of the park to the Lake Hotel in a furious rainstorm. Dusk was setting in and he could only see a few feet ahead of him; he slowed down knowing it was just a few miles to the hotel. Coming around a curve, he spotted a shape in the road — it was a woman in a long old-fashioned dress.

Todd quickly stopped the car, asking the poor, drenched girl if she needed a ride. She quickly jumped in and thanked him. Todd offered her his coat to keep the chill off her and asked what she was doing out in such a storm. She replied she was from Gardiner and worked as a waitress at the Canyon Inn. Struck with her beauty, Todd continued inquiring about her. Her name was Victoria Vendables and her old-fashioned dress was her uniform. It seems she was waiting for her ride to work, but it had never showed up. It was not long before they pulled up to the Canyon Inn; Victoria thanked the young man and hurried off to get to work.

Todd continued on to his destination, but could not stop thinking about the lovely lady he had shared his car with that evening. Determined to see her again, he asked around the next day if anyone knew of the girl. No one recognized her name, but, much to his surprise, it was also revealed that the Canyon Inn had burned down years earlier. Todd had to find out for himself; after all, he was just there the previous night. As he pulled up to where the hotel should have been, he wondered if he could have taken a wrong turn. However, this could not be so, as he remembered the drive up. However, the hotel was nothing but a foundation now.

He thought back to the old-fashioned dress the girl wore and, no, it could not be... Was she a ghost? Todd lazily drove around the roads, wondering who the girl was he had met the night before and what had happened to his jacket. Just around a bend in the road, he came upon the Army Cemetery. Walking among the headstones, he noticed one had his jacket folded neatly under it: Miss Victoria Vendables died July 22, 1914, from pneumonia, age thirty-five; she was a waitress at the Canyon Hotel.

Yellowstone Lake

The closest anyone has come to explaining the mystery of the singing lake is escaping volcanic gases, or a far off flock of geese taking flight. "So far no one has the faintest proof of what causes them," claims J. M. Good, former chief naturalist.

The mysterious singing has been described as "the ringing of telegraph wires or the hum of bees, beginning softly in the distance, growing rapidly plainer until directly overhead, and then fading rapidly in the opposite direction," explains Max Bauer, geologist and former chief naturalist at the park. Other visitors to the park describe the sound as a giant pipe organ echoing in the distance.

To listen to the singing, visit Yellowstone Lake on cloudless, windless, mornings for optimum sound, but the singing has been reported to occur at other times of the day and other kinds of weather.

The mysterious sounds have been coming from the lake since the first explorer happened upon the lake. One spooky account describes the sound as "the faint sound of voices answering each other overhead." American Indians believe that spirits inhabit the lake and the sounds you hear, whether organ bells or bees humming, are the spirits communicating.

SIGHTINGS

The Great Spirit

A legend explains about a great flood that protected Yellowstone from destruction by the hand of man. Recounted to Professor Hap Gilliland of Eastern Montana College, he was the first to record this legend. "The Great Spirit smiled on this land when he made it. There were mountains and plains, forests and grasslands. There were animals of many kinds—and men."

The Great Spirit told the people, "These animals are your brothers. Share the land with them. They will give you food and clothing. Live with them and protect them.

"Protect especially the buffalo, for the buffalo will give you food and shelter. The hide of the buffalo will keep you from the cold, from the heat, and from the rain. As long as you have the buffalo, you will never need to suffer."

For many winters the people lived at peace with the animals and with the land. When they killed a buffalo, they thanked the Great Spirit, and they used every part of the buffalo. It took care of every need.

Then other people came. They did not think of the animals as brothers. They killed, even when they did not need food. They burned and cut the forests, and the animals died. They shot the buffalo and called it sport. They killed the fish in the streams.

When the Great Spirit looked down, he was sad. He let the smoke of the fires lie in the valleys. The people coughed and choked, but still they burned and they killed.

So the Great Spirit sent rains to put out the fires and to destroy the people.

The rains fell, and the waters rose. The people moved from the flooded valleys to the higher land.

Spotted Bear, the Medicine Man, gathered together his people. He said to them, "The Great Spirit has told us that as long as we have the buffalo we will be safe from heat and cold and rain, but there are no longer any buffalo. Unless we can find buffalo and live at peace with nature, we will all die."

Still the rains fell, and the waters rose. The people moved from the flooded plains to the hills.

The young men went out and hunted for the buffalo. As they went, they put out the fires. They made friends with the animals once more. They cleaned out the streams.

Still the rains fell, and the waters rose. The people moved from the flooded hills to the mountains.

Two young men came to Spotted Bear. "We have found the buffalo," they said. "There was a cow, a calf, and a great white bull. The cow and the calf climbed up to the safety of the mountains. They should be back when the rain stops, but the bank gave way and the bull was swept away by the floodwaters. We followed and got him to shore, but he had drowned. We have brought you his hide."

They unfolded a huge white buffalo skin.

Spotted Bear took the white buffalo hide. "Many people have been drowned," he said. "Our food has been carried away, but our young people are no longer destroying the world that was created for them. They have found the white buffalo. It will save those who are left."

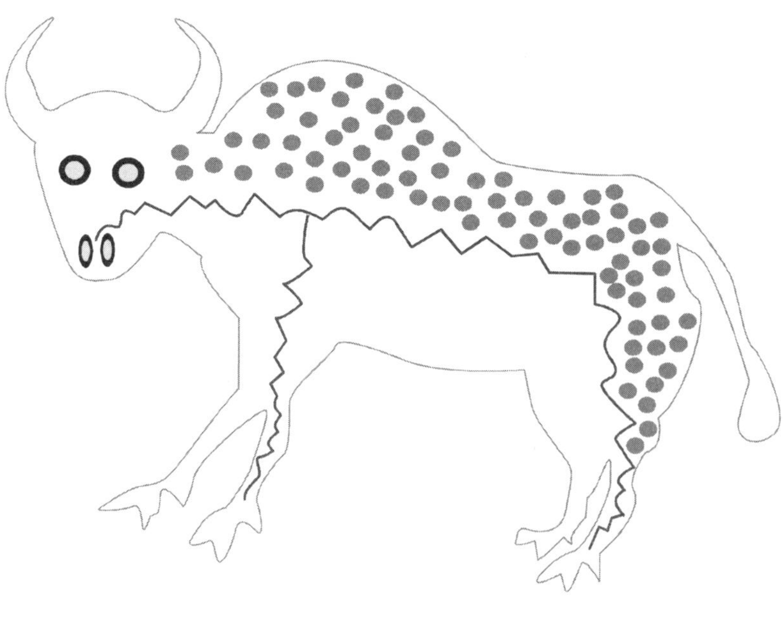

Still the rains fell, and the waters rose. The people moved from the flooded mountains to the highest peaks.

Spotted Bear spread the white buffalo skin on the ground. He and the other medicine men scraped it and stretched it, and scraped it and stretched it.

Still the rains fell. Like all rawhide, the buffalo skin stretched when it was wet. Spotted Bear stretched it out over the village. All the people who were left crowded under it.

As the rains fell, the medicine men stretched the buffalo skin across the mountains. Each day they stretched it farther.

Then Spotted Bear tied one corner to the top of the Big Horn Mountains. That side, he fastened to the Pryors. The next corner he tied to the Bear Tooth Mountains. Crossing the Yellowstone Valley, he tied one corner to the Crazy Mountains, and the other to Signal Butte in the Bull Mountains.

The whole Yellowstone Valley was covered by the white buffalo skin. Though the rains still fell above, it did not fall in the Yellowstone Valley.

The waters sank away. Animals from the outside moved into the valley and under the white buffalo skin. The people shared the valley with them.

Still the rains fell above the buffalo skin. The skin stretched and began to sag.

Spotted Bear stood on the Bridger Mountains and raised the west end of the buffalo skin to catch the West Wind. The West Wind rushed in and was caught under the buffalo skin. The wind lifted the skin until it formed a great dome over the valley.

The Great Spirit saw that the people were living at peace with the earth. The rains stopped, and the sun shone. As the sun shone on the white buffalo skin, it gleamed with colors of red and yellow and blue.

Indians chose to leap to their fate from the Lower Falls in Yellowstone.
Courtesy of R. W. O'Brien.

Lower Falls

The Crow Indians believed Yellowstone Lake and the geysers surrounding it were possessed with evil spirits. Furthermore, the head of Yellowstone River was the end of the world. If the Indians were to climb to the top of the mountains, they would see into another world — the spirit world.

When the white settlers came and drove the Indians out, many of them chose rather than being slaughtered by the white men for not leaving to go over the Lower Falls of the Yellowstone River to their certain death. They climbed into their raft and chanted, as the white men watched, a "mournful dirge." Today you can hear their chant near the bottom of the falls in the mist that rises up.

Disappearance of Mrs. Trischman

Mrs. Trischman had high hopes when her husband secured a new job at Yellowstone Park. She had just been released from a Bozeman psychiatry hospital for slashing her own throat with a butcher knife. However, after only four days surrounded by her children she had another fit. Grabbing her five-year-old son, Joseph, she nearly decapitated him with a hunting knife. The children frantically rushed to their neighbor's house for safety.

At once the neighbor, upon hearing of what had just transpired, hurried to Mrs. Trischman's house. Mrs. Trischman was sitting quietly as if nothing had occurred. She further claimed to have no recollection of what had just happened.

Mrs. Trischman was then locked up in the Old Guardhouse for her and everyone else's safety until she could be safely transported to a mental ward in Washington D.C. A few days later the train pulled into the station and Mrs. Trischman boarded without incident. The train did not get far before it was halted. It seems Mrs. Trischman had jumped from the moving train, falling into the Yellowstone River and vanishing forever. The authorities searched for her, but they found no sign of the woman. To this day, it is still not known what happened to Mrs. Trischman.

SIGHTINGS

Bigfoot

Throughout the years there have been many sightings of Bigfoot in Wyoming. Though most of them have been in the Yellowstone area, there have been several in other parts of Wyoming that you would not expect.

The most recent sighting reported to the Bigfoot Field Researchers Organization was in the fall of 2008. Several campers at a remote campsite in the Medicine Bow National Forest encountered what they describe as a dark figure running quickly between a tent and one of the vehicles at their campsite. The night before the campers had heard rustling in the bushes nearby and felt as if something was watching them.

In the same forest a few years earlier a bow hunter was out looking for game when he ran across a large upright animal about three hundred yards in front of him. The hunter described the animal as being around eight feet tall and very hairy. Losing sight of the large animal in the fog, the hunter went back to his business. A few days later, the hunter heard a "terrible scream like nothing I had ever heard before." Did the hunter encounter Bigfoot in the Medicine Bow National Forest?

In another part of the state, two hikers came across a small family of Bigfoots looking curiously at their truck in 1998. The two men were coming back from a hike; it was now about 8 p.m. and the sun had set, but the moon was lighting up the area for them well enough to see where to go. As they approached their vehicle, they noticed two large upright hairy creatures and one smaller one looking at their truck. The men were able to observe the creatures for a few seconds before the hairy beasts noticed them and ran off into the woods. Neither of the men spoke a word of this incident again fearing that no one would believe them.

Yellowstone has more than a few stories from park rangers and visitors about seeing Bigfoot. One ranger who rides the back country

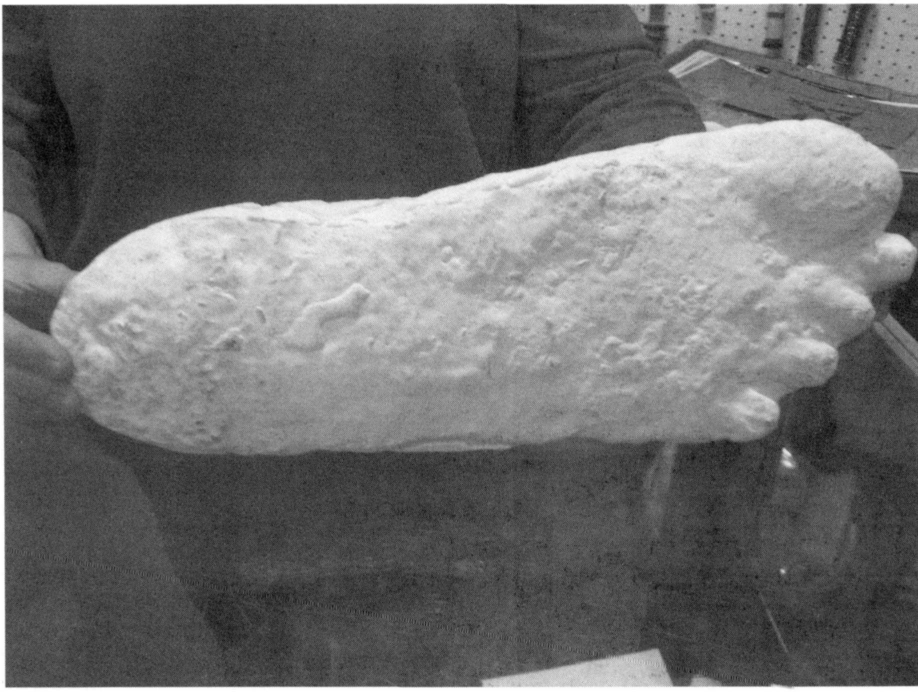

Bigfoot still roams Yellowstone National Park.

on horseback came upon Bigfoot one afternoon. He described the creature as being smart and looking for cover to hide from the ranger. As the animal ran off, he was reaching down, grabbing for objects to throw at the ranger.

After the ranger's experience, he started asking around Jackson if anyone had experiences or heard strange vocalizations. A crew out in the park examining the blister rust on the white bark pine had come across a deboned elk with large human-like footprints near it. Around the same time, they also heard unearthly howls coming out of the nearby woods. Many other outdoor enthusiasts came forward and said they also had heard unknown screams and howls from the woods.

When people think of Bigfoot, they think of the Pacific Northwest. Northern California is famous for its Bigfoot sightings, as well as the coast of Oregon and Washington State. Not many people think that Bigfoot would be roaming the hills and valleys of Wyoming. When you are exploring Wyoming and Yellowstone National Park, make sure to keep one eye open for Bigfoot... He might be closer than you think.

Old Faithful Inn

Old Faithful Village, Old Faithful
Yellowstone National Park, Wyoming
(307) 344-7901
yellowstonenationalparklodges.com

The Old Faithful Inn is the largest log structure in the world with a 65-foot lobby. The massive structure was designed by 29-year-old Robert C. Reamer, who wanted the lodge to reflect and blend in with the natural environment. Reamer successfully provided visitors to Yellowstone with a "western experience." The Northern Pacific Railroad, with the cost of around $165,000, funded the original construction of the hotel. In 1903, the 'Old House' was finished including the dining room, kitchen wings, and two guest wings. In 1913, the east wing was built and, in 1927, the west wing was built.

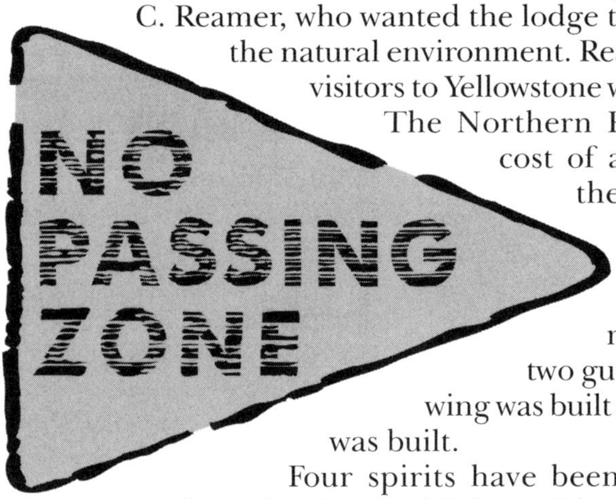

Four spirits have been documented within the walls of the Old Faithful Inn. The most famous is that of the headless bride. She was a mere fifteen years old when she fell in love with a servant who worked for her father, a wealthy businessman. Her father saw the much older man as an opportunist and forbid his daughter from seeing him. She refused and threatened her father that she would run off with the man if she could not marry him. Not wanting a scandal, the couple was allowed to marry in a quiet ceremony and sent to Yellowstone on their honeymoon. The young girl was given a large lump sum of money to survive on until her new husband could procure work for himself.

The first day at the Inn was filled with sightseeing and to onlookers the couple seemed happy and in love. That night the

Yellowstone Lodge is home to a decapitated bride looking for her head. *Courtesy of R. W. O'Brien.*

girl found out her new husband had gambled away all their money and they had nothing to live on. Her husband insisted she send a wire to her father asking for more money. Her father refused and cut off his daughter completely from the family if she stayed with this man. Upon returning to her room and explaining the situation to her new husband, an explosive fight ensued, and her husband fled the hotel.

A day or two passed and the staff of the hotel had not seen the young girl. Thinking that she was grieving, they wanted to give her space. Now they were beginning to worry. After knocking she did not answer the door. The staff opened the door and found the young woman in the bathtub filled with blood. Her lifeless body bloated and discolored revealed that she had been decapitated. After an exhausting search, her head was found in the Crow's Nest of the hotel.

Ever since that time, the young woman has been seen climbing the stairs to the crow's nest retrieving her head and descending the stairs with her head tucked under her arm. If you are brave enough to wander the hotel late at night after everyone is silently sleeping, you may just run into the headless bride.

The second spirit that resides at the Old Faithful Inn is that of a lost little boy. As you stand overlooking the great hall, a little boy may approach you with tears streaming down his face. The scared little boy is always wearing a T-shirt, shorts, and tennis shoes; he does not speak beyond telling you that he cannot find his mother and father. Many guests have taken his little hand in theirs and walked down to the main desk. After explaining they found this little boy lost, the clerk and guest turn to look at the boy, but he has mysteriously vanished.

Some employees of the Old Faithful Inn claim that Reamer still walks the halls of the masterpiece he spent so much time working on. Reamer was just twenty-nine when he was commissioned to design the Old Faithful Inn and numerous other structures in the Yellowstone National Park. Just as work was finishing up on the Inn, Reamer's wife died of Bright's disease. Reamer was distraught and turned to alcoholism. His family thought it was best if he returned home and after a few years Reamer moved to Seattle and married his second wife, the niece of Yellowstone's commissioner. In 1926, Reamer returned to Yellowstone and expanded the Old Faithful Inn. Just ten years later Reamer's second wife died of Ovarian cancer. Once again distraught he returned to Seattle and on January 7, 1938 Reamer died of a heart attack.

A short man in an old-fashioned black hat has been seen wandering the halls of the Inn. Has Reamer returned to the place he loved most or is he watching over the hotel he painstakingly designed, making sure that it is still a masterpiece.

The final ghost that has been seen at the hotel is that of an older sailor. He is best-known for rattling door knobs and shaking windows in the guest rooms. His spirit has been seen wandering quietly down the hallways; other times he is seen peering through windows as if he is looking for someone or something and impatiently waiting. What is he looking for?

One couple at the hotel had an unnerving experience one night in their room. Exhausted from their day's adventures, they plopped down in bed, hastily pulled the covers up, and immediately fell asleep. In the middle of the night, the couple awoke naked and bare of all bed linens. The room was blustery with heat. They leapt out of bed and noticed all their clothes and linens were folded neatly at the bottom of their bed. The man went to the radiator to turn off the heat, but the radiator was cold and untouched. Did the spirit of the sailor find their room unlocked and play a prank on the frightened guests, or was this another of the Inn's spirits' tricks?

The Old Faithful Inn's beauty and proximity to the famous geyser is a must-see when visiting Yellowstone National Park, but beware while you wander the halls or stay the night at the historic hotel. You may just get more than you bargained for while visiting the Inn.

Jackson

Jackson is a tourist stop for visitors to Yellowstone National Park as well as the Grand Teton National Park. The town is known more as Jackson Hole: in 1886, the town was sucked into an underground lake, and today the name still sticks.

Jackson got its start as a trading post. Its great location lured trappers into homesteading in the area. Soon the town was thriving with the opening of Yellowstone and Grand Teton. Ranching was the main source of income for residents of Jackson in the early years; now the town is devoted to tourism.

The Wort Hotel

Glenwood & Broadway
Jackson, Wyoming 83001
(307) 733-2190
www.worthotel.com

Charles Wort homesteaded in the Jackson area. He owned a livery stable and was an outfitter for the upper crust of society. He soon saw the need for a hotel to house these members of society, and to create a meeting place other than his drafty, cold livery stable for the townsfolk. Unfortunately, Charles died in 1933 before his dream could come to be.

Charles had two sons, Jonathan and Jess, who owned a few parcels of land in the Grand Teton National Park. In 1940, the Wort brothers sold their land for the large sum of $90,000 and built their father's dream.

The grand hotel opened for business in 1941, offering the town of Jackson a meeting place and a luxury place for the best of society to sleep. In 1950, the world-famous Silver Dollar bar opened for business featuring a bar inlaid with 2,032 silver dollars. It was not long before actors filming in the area found the hotel. Allen Ladd and Jean Arthur stayed at the Wort while filming the movie *Shane*.

More than the maintenance man haunts this beautiful Wort Hotel. *Courtesy of R. W. O'Brien.*

Henry Fonda, Clark Gable, and Glenn Ford also spent time sleeping under the roof of the hotel.

For many years the hotel offered guests gambling; though illegal in Wyoming, officials often looked the other way. Gambling was so lucrative the Wort Brothers earned back the money they spent building and decorating the hotel within two years of the opening. The hotel offered guests craps, poker, roulette, and other illegal activities within its walls. It was such big business the brothers employed a lookout. Sitting high on Teton Pass the spotter could see when the federal authorities were coming and alert the Wort. Tables and games would be quickly sequestered. The games continued well into the 1960s.

In 1980, the hotel caught fire. The whole town came out for the event. The firemen gave rocks to the children watching to throw through the windows on the upper floor to help. Fortunately only the second floor of the hotel was lost. The first floor of the hotel was saved from the ravishes of the flames and the Silver Dollar bar was untouched. The next day the local newspaper wrote an obituary about the loss of the hotel. Immediately the hotel was rebuilt and in 2003 new owners bought The Wort and began restoration. Preserving and improving the grand hotel and meeting place is the passion of the new owners and today the hotel stands magnificent as ever.

Now that you know a bit about the history and lore of the hotel, let me tell you about the ghost that loves the hotel just as much as the guests and employees, and one that seems lost within its walls.

Robert Tomingas was the maintenance man at the hotel starting in the 1950s. Bob loved the hotel and was considered a mechanical genius. Living in an apartment in the basement of the hotel, he would fix the impossible. Bob would comment that he witnessed several supernatural events including doors opening and closing and water faucets turning on and off by themselves. Since Bob passed away, fellow maintenance men and employees at The Wort have claimed projects finish or fix themselves. Breezes move about the hotel on wintery days when the hotel is shut tight. Bob is still hanging around the hotel he loved so much in life, fixing the impossible and keeping watch over the structure.

Claudia the head concierge at The Wort recounted that several times on her way down the stairs to the basement a box would appear out of nowhere. Once the box fell from above her out of thin air and landed at her feet. On another occasion the same box she saw earlier was sitting near the bottom of the steps as she returned to go up the stairs. Where did the box come from? She thinks Bob is sending her a message, but as to what the message is it is still unknown.

Another spirit that has been seen occasionally at the hotel is that of a little girl. She is spotted mainly on the second floor and usually heads around the corner; when guests and employees go looking for her, she has disappeared.

No one knows for sure how many ghosts reside at The Wort Hotel, but I can assure you many of the employees have a story to tell about Bob... Why don't you visit and see for yourself?

Directions To Teton Mystery Spot: From Wort Hotel, head west on US-191 South toward North Millward Street. Turn left at Horse Creek Road. Your destination will be on the Left.

Teton Mystery Spot

9800 South US Highway 89
Jackson, Wyoming 83001

There are a handful of strange places across the country where brooms stand up, balls roll up hill, and you can walk on walls. Many people think these sites are hoaxes and many of them are, but if you can find the few that are not it is worth the trip.

You may ask if there is something paranormal going on at these sites, and yes, if you agree that paranormal is something other than normal. One theory claims a large metal cone was placed under the ground by aliens creating the anomalies in gravity. Another theory is that a great beam of "high velocity soft electrons" flows from the earth through a vortex of energy. One man thought that time speeds up and slows down. John Lister studied the Oregon Vortex for over forty years and burned all his research before his death claiming, "The world isn't ready for what goes on here." If you have time check out this spot, is it aliens, vortexes, or just a trick?

Conclusion

Wyoming is full of wide open spaces, hidden nooks, and national parks that are rivaled by none. As you venture through the least populated state in the United States, remember spirits are around every corner.

Jackalopes play on the prairies, sing old cowboy songs, and drink your whiskey while you are sleeping. Little people live in the hills and clear your fields. The shoes you come across at the discount store might just have been made from Big Nose George. In addition, if you see a ship coming out of a heavy fog, a loved one may be next to die.

In *Haunted Wyoming*, I have tried to take you on an adventure into the unknown, haunted abodes, spooky neighborhoods, and the underbelly of lore and legend located within the state. When you find yourself in one of these places, make sure to take lots of photographs. Be still and observe...and you too may have your own story to tell by the end of your journey.

As a final note, I cannot stress enough to be respectful of the spirits and living alike. No one wants a run-in with the law or worse. If you get scared, don't run — calmly walk away from the area to a safe place where you will not get hurt.

Have a spooky good time on your journey into *Haunted Wyoming*.

Appendix
Guide for Urban Exploration

This guide was written by and offered courtesy of Scott Lefebvre, author of Spooky Creepy Long Island

Things You Might Want to Bring Along

Light

If your planned destination is a building, day or night, you'll want to bring a flashlight. If you enter an abandoned building, there will most likely be rooms that do not have direct access to the outside and will be dark without artificial light. It's also important to always be able to see where you're going. The most common injuries for urban explorers are tripping over something underfoot because they weren't watching where they were going, or hitting their head, or getting cut by something hanging down from overhead.

My favorite flashlight is the Mag-Lite mini. It's more expensive than the one-use flashlights that you can buy at the register or get for free as a promotional item with a pack of batteries, but it's infinitely more reliable and durable. It will survive a few accidental drops onto concrete floors, and the bulbs are cheap and replaceable. The light it throws is bright, clear, and adjustable, and it's relatively cheap, so it won't be a big deal if you drop it someplace that you can't easily retrieve it. It runs on double AA's and gets pretty good battery life, but make sure you bring spare batteries. You don't want to be trapped in an unfamiliar, potentially dangerous environment with a handful of dead flashlights.

Photography

A camera with a good flash is also highly recommended. Digital cameras are lighter and often cheaper than film cameras and can take a lot of pictures without requiring the user to play around with loading in a new roll of film in a dusty, musty environment. Plus, if you have to run, you don't want a bulky film camera with a flash attachment bumping around. Some of the most common sad stories about urban exploration are about broken or lost film cameras. Don't be one of those people.

Hair

Tying back long hair and wearing a baseball hat is recommended. You don't want your hair to accidentally get snagged on something and get pulled out. If you're going to hit your head on something, it's better to get your hat knocked off than to get a rusty cut. Additionally, a stray hair flashed in front of a camera lens is frequently mistaken for evidence of the presence of the supernatural. A common and embarrassing error, and easily avoidable with a little precaution.

Attire

Wear sensible shoes: sneakers with thick, skid-proof soles, or even better, work boots. The floors of abandoned buildings are often cluttered with debris and filth and sometimes damp or flooded. Also keep in mind that you may have to avoid wild animals or other hazards, so please be smart and tie your shoes. Only run if you're outside. Even a familiar spot might have changed since the last time you were there. Running in an unfamiliar environment is easily the best way to accidentally and possibly seriously hurt yourself while urban exploring.

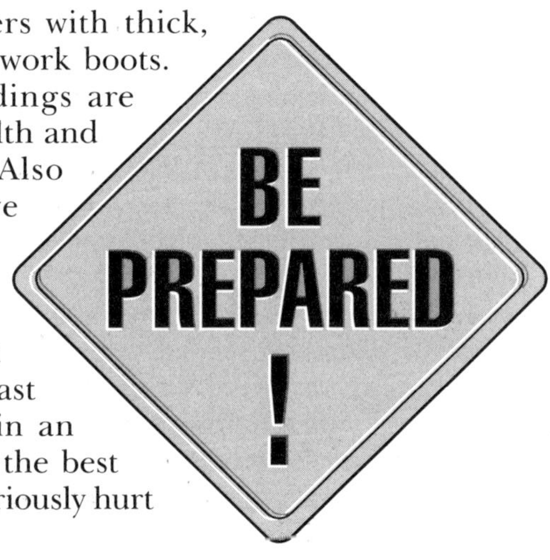

You may want to bring light work gloves. Not so much to avoid leaving fingerprints, but more because abandoned buildings can be dirty places. There are rusty ladders and stairwell handrails and the walls are usually moldy. Anywhere you put your hands you can pick up dirt and you don't want that kind of dirt in your eyes or mouth. It's better to get your glove snagged on something sharp instead of cutting your hand open.

Just for Your Health

Speaking of mold and dust, if you're predisposed to allergies, you may want to invest in a good dust mask. In some old buildings, there's lead paint dust and asbestos.

The Legalities

We all know that trespassing is illegal. If you're uncomfortable with possible legal involvement, there are many excellent places of supernatural interest that are perfectly legal to visit and explore.

It's important to keep in mind that even going onto a property that is not public can be considered trespassing. If you enter an abandoned building, that can be considered illegal entry and trespassing — and if you had to do anything to a window or door to get into a building, it becomes breaking and entering.

Also, I implore you *not* to bring any weapons along with you while urban exploring. Having a small pocketknife or pocket multi-tool like a Swiss Army knife or a Leatherman can be convenient and handy, especially if your hair or clothes get snagged and you have to cut yourself loose, but it's completely unnecessary to bring a big hunting knife, or even worse, a handgun. If you're looking for ghosts, a weapon won't do you any good against them. Having a weapon just makes it that much more likely someone will accidentally get hurt, and being discovered while urban exploring just gets more complicated if you're running around with a samurai sword.

Please be smart, be safe, and send me a set of your awesome pictures — or even better, take me along on your next trip.

Ghost Hunting Glossary

There are many words that ghost hunters use in reference to ghosts and haunted places. You're probably familiar with most of these words, but some may be new or have different meanings when they refer to haunted places. The following information is provided by ghost investigator, Fiona Broome, and appears in her book, Ghosts of Austin, Texas.

Afterlife

One of several terms used interchangeably to refer to life after death, the word "afterlife" has been used since 1615. It is generic enough to use in almost any setting and culture. Other popular terms include "crossing over," "the Otherworld," and "the other side." Most ghost hunters avoid specific religious terms such as "heaven" and "the Summerland" when discussing ghosts, hauntings, and the afterlife.

Aliens

This is the term we give visitors from other planets. We differentiate aliens from visitors that live in parallel worlds, the Otherworld, or what's generally characterized as the afterlife. Some ghost hunters believe in UFOs and aliens; others don't. Generally, ghost hunters don't mix the two studies.

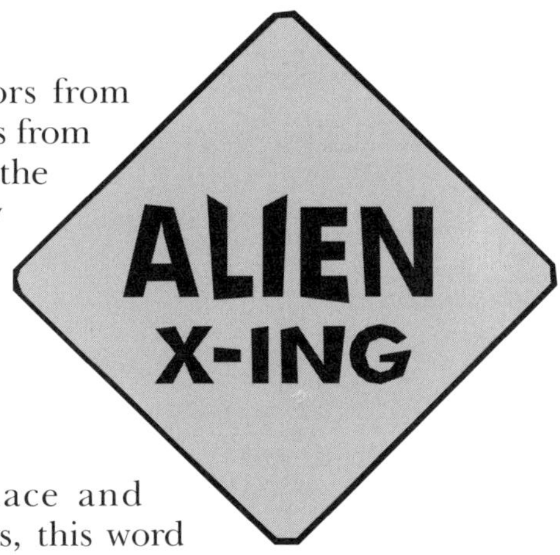

Anomaly

Something that is out of place and unexplained; in paranormal studies, this word refers to any phenomena that we cannot explain. Example: A lens flare in a photo is not an anomaly if you can see the light source that created it, but an orb that cannot be explained is an anomaly.

Apparition

Since the early seventeenth century, this word has referred to a ghost that seems to have a material substance. If it appears in any physical form, including a vapor-like image, it may be called an apparition.

Banshee

This word comes from the Irish, bean sidhe, meaning female spirit. Most families with Irish ancestors have at least one banshee story if you do enough research, but many people are reluctant to discuss this subject. Her wail does not always mean death. She does not cause anyone to die. She's generally not a ghost.

Clearing, or Space Clearing

This is a process of ridding an area of lingering unpleasant energy. It does not "kill" a ghost. Space clearing may encourage ghosts to cross over, or at least leave the haunted location.

Immediately after a space clearing, ghosts can be noisier or more hostile than usual. An effective space clearing may take three to five days to work. In the most haunted settings, it's usually necessary to repeat the space clearing several times.

Demons

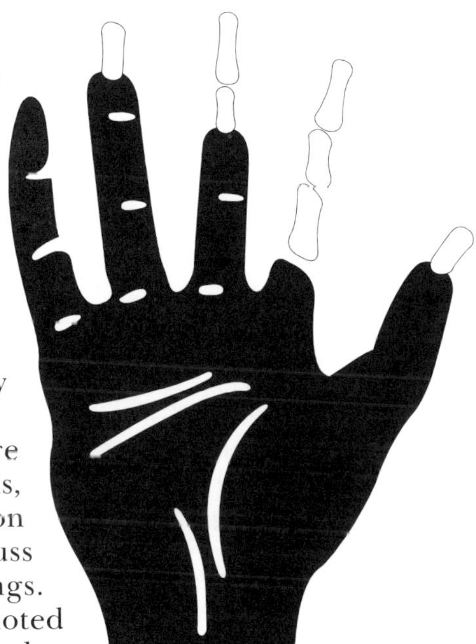

Historically, this term has included deceased individuals. However, since the early eighteenth century, the word "demon" usually refers to an evil spirit, sometimes more powerful than man, but less than a Deity. Today, we generally do not use this term to indicate a deceased human being. The female demon, very rarely mentioned, is a demoness.

Demons and possessions are treated like UFOs and aliens. That is, most ghost hunters have an opinion about them, but they rarely discuss them in connection with hauntings. The "Amityville Horror" is one noted exception where the story seemed to include both ghosts and possessions.

However, ghosts generally do not attempt to take over a living body. In most cases, they believe they are still alive and, in their minds, that each still has his or her own body. They're not interested in anyone else's.

Doppelganger

A concept made popular in the early nineteenth century, especially by Shelley and Byron, the doppelganger is the apparition, or double, of a living person. This may be a paranormal phenomenon, but it's not a ghost. It does not forecast anything tragic.

Dowsing rods

These are usually single rods, split rods, or L-shaped wires or twigs. Some people dowse with pendulums, too. They're popularly used to locate water and oil wells, and to measure energy levels of many kinds. For ghost research, we usually use two L-shaped rods.

In ghost hunting, the investigator loosely carries one rod in each hand and watches the movement of the rods. When the rods cross or splay wide apart, it usually indicates a haunted location.

It's easy to make your own dowsing rods from a coat hanger wire. Cut the wire near the top, and again at the opposite end of the lower section. Do this with two different coat hangers to create two dowsing rods. You can also purchase ready-made dowsing rods. Be certain that they're long enough for ghost research; the 16-inch length is recommended. Look for dowsing tools that glow in the dark. They're especially useful for ghost hunting.

Hold each one loosely in your hands with your arms extended or your elbows bent at a right angle. The rods should be pointed straight ahead of you, and able to swing on their own. If the rods are drifting, this could be from the normal movement of your body. However, in haunted places, the pull on the rods is strong and cannot be mistaken for a casual, unconscious movement of your hands. When you step out of the haunted area, the rods return to their original position.

Some researchers successfully use dowsing rods to find unmarked graves. With practice, it's possible to use the rods to detect other information about the body in the grave and the spirit that may haunt the site.

Ectoplasm

Often referred to as "ecto," this is the physical residue of psychic energy. It's the basis for "slime" used in the *Ghostbusters* movies. Ectoplasm can be seen by the naked eye and is best viewed in dark settings, since it is translucent and tends to glow. It is very unusual. Researchers often describe it as a vivid, *The X-Files* kind of lime green. It usually fades from sight gradually.

EMF

The initials stand for Electro Magnetic Field or Electro Magnetic Frequency. In the broadest terms, EMF is a combination of electrical and magnetic fields. You'll find EMF around power sources, including fuse boxes, electrical outlets, computer monitors, and microwave ovens. It would be smart to study EMF so that you recognize the normal sources of elevated EMF readings. Constant, clearly defined EMF fields usually have a logical explanation. Unexplained EMF fields may indicate something paranormal. EMF fields can be measured with various tools, including an EMF meter or a hiking compass.

Entity

An entity is any being, including people, animals, and ghosts. It can also refer to aliens, faeries, mystical beasts, and a wide range of paranormal creatures. If you use this term — and many ghost hunters do — be sure that others understand your context.

ESP

The abbreviation for Extra Sensory Perception, it means the ability to perceive things beyond the usual five senses of smell, hearing, touch, taste, and sight. Although these perceptions may be interpreted as sounds or sights, experienced ghost hunters can usually tell the difference between normal detection with the five senses and things detected with the "sixth sense" or psychic abilities.

EVP

Meaning Electronic Voice Phenomena, this is the recording of unexplained voices, usually in haunted settings. Sometimes the voices are heard during the investigation. More often, though, the voices are whispers, understood only when a sound recording is processed, filtered, and amplified with a computer.

When people first recorded EVPs, they insisted on total silence so normal noises and talking wouldn't be confused with an EVP. More recently, people have deliberately included sounds such as normal talking and white noise. Some researchers believe that ghosts may need ambient noise to create their own sounds and speech.

Most researchers use digital recorders to save EVPs. Once the researcher is at home, he or she uses a computer program to filter out everyday noises, such as airplanes and passing cars. The recording may need to be speeded up or slowed down, or a range of sounds magnified above others.

Faeries

Beings that live in the Otherworld or Underworld parallel to our world and not far from it. Many researchers who readily accept the reality of ghosts don't believe in faeries. Similar to the subject of aliens and UFOs, it's best to keep faerie research clearly separated from your ghost hunting.

Fear

Most ghost hunters have a healthy respect for ghosts and paranormal phenomena. Many ghost hunters enjoy a "good scare." However, if you feel genuinely alarmed or frightened while ghost hunting, it's prudent to leave that location. It may have been your imagination, but there may be something (or someone) truly dangerous nearby.

Ghost hunting should always be interesting, and sometimes entertaining. If it's not, you may be at risk. Ghost hunting should never become a "dare" or an endurance test. If you're truly frightened in any setting — haunted or not — leave immediately. If this happens regularly when you're ghost hunting, choose a different hobby.

Ghost

This is the term given to a sentient entity or spirit that visits or lingers in our world after he or she lived among us as a human being. We've also seen evidence of ghostly animals and pets.

Ghoul

This word has been mistakenly used to mean a ghost. "Ghoul" comes from Middle Eastern lore, where it may refer to an evil spirit that robs graves.

Haunted

The description given a setting where ghosts, poltergeists, and/or residual energy seem to produce significant paranormal activity, the word "haunt" originally meant "to frequent."

Medium

This word usually refers to something in the middle, relative to size or duration. In ghost hunting, it means anyone who is able to convey communications from departed spirits or a person who is able to maintain a position between the world of the living and those who have crossed over and talk with (or for) those on the other side.

This term was popularized in the mid-nineteenth century and is often used interchangeably with the word "psychic." Some people call themselves psychic mediums because they can communicate with the other side, but also sense other paranormal energy and/or work with ESP.

Occult

From the Latin, meaning something that is concealed or covered. Since the sixteenth century, it has meant anything that is mysterious. Today in America, it generally refers to magical, mystical and experimental studies.

Orb

An orb is a round, whitish or pastel-colored translucent area in photos. Generally, these are perfectly circular, not oval. Many researchers believe that they represent spirits or ghosts.

If you're using a digital camera, it's important to differentiate between an area of broken pixels (called an "artifact") and the translucent, circular image that is an orb. Also, any reflective surface or light source can create a lens flare that looks like an orb. When taking photos, note any glass, shiny metal, reflective signs, or polished surfaces such as tables, headstones, and lights.

In most cases, ghost hunters do not see orbs when they're at a haunted site. Usually, orbs show up only in photos. They are the most common evidence for hauntings.

Ouija

From the French and German words for "yes," this is a spelling board used with a planchette. The device is intended to communicate with and through the spirit world, obtaining answers to questions.

Generally, we don't recommend them on serious ghost investigations. Some people are vehemently opposed to Ouija boards. The biggest problem is that researchers can't tell who is really moving the planchette. Even if it is a ghost, the spirit could be playing a prank or lying; the information from Ouija boards is unreliable for ghost research.

Paranormal

The prefix "para" indicates something that is irregular, faulty, or operating outside the usual boundaries, so "paranormal" refers to anything outside the realm and experiences that we consider normal.

Parapsychology

The study of mental abilities and effects outside the usual realm of psychology. Parapsychology includes the study of ESP, ghosts, luck, psychokinesis, and other paranormal phenomena.

Pendulum

A small weight at the end of a cord or chain that is usually about six to ten inches long. The movement of the weight, when uninfluenced by other factors, can be used to detect areas of paranormal energy.

Poltergeist

From the German meaning "noisy ghost," this term has been in use since the early nineteenth century to mean a spirit that makes noise or otherwise plays annoying pranks. Unlike other ghosts, poltergeists can move from one location to another, following the person they've chosen to torment. Many psychologists believe that poltergeists are not ghosts at all, but some form of psychokinesis or remote activity, usually related to a teenager.

Portal

Literally a doorway or gate, this term suggests a specific location through which spirits enter and leave our world. When there are multiple phenomena in a confined area, such as an abundance of unexplained orbs, some people call this a "ghost portal."

Possession

When an entity attempts to take control of a body that does not belong to them, it's called a possession. In ghost hunting, this phenomenon is rare, but some psychics and mediums allow ghosts to speak through them. Sometimes, this can enable the living to communicate directly with the ghost and help him or her to cross over.

In extreme cases, a spirit can maliciously attempt to takeover an unwilling person's body. Most ghost hunters will never witness this kind of possession, though it's a popular and common scene in horror movies. Unwilling possession is often linked to demonic activity.

Protection

Some researchers use objects, rituals, routines, tactics, or specific processes to protect themselves against ghostly, demonic, or paranormal intrusions and effects. This is a personal matter and rarely discussed during a ghost hunt.

When you go on a ghost hunt, it's generally smart to carry something that you feel may protect you from evil. Most ghost hunters wear a small cross, Star of David, pentacle, or other religious jewelry. They often conceal it under clothing or wear it as a ring, earrings, or on a bracelet where it won't be noticed. Carrying a very big, heavy Bible, an intimidating (and very visible) athame, or a large religious icon is usually considered excessive.

Psi

"Psi" or "psy" is a popular term used to mean any psychic phenomenon or psychic ability, and is sometimes inclusive of paranormal disturbances.

Psychic

From the Greek word meaning "of the soul" or "of life" (Paul used it in the Bible, I Cor ii, 14), this word usually refers to the world outside the domain of physical law. "Psychic" can relate to the spirit or the mind, depending upon the context. When someone is described as a psychic, it usually means that he or she is able to perceive things that are outside traditional physical laws and perceptions.

Psychical

A British term used as an adjective or adverb for what Americans call "psychic."

Psychokinesis or Psycho Kinesis

To move something with the powers of one's mind, this could be a factor in some hauntings and particularly in poltergeist phenomena. It's also called "PK." *(See telekinesis)*

Residual Energy

Many ghost hunters believe that emotionally-charged events leave an imprint or residue on the physical objects nearby. What distinguishes residual energy from an active haunting is that the energy/impressions repeat consistently, as if on a tape loop. The energy level may increase or decrease, but the content remains the same with each manifestation. By contrast, in an active haunting, the ghost may respond to environmental stimuli and direct contact.

Sixth Sense

Since normal phenomena are detected with the five senses (smell, taste, touch, hearing, and sight), anything that you experience outside those five senses may be categorized as a sixth sense. Usually, this indicates to psychic detection or ESP.

Since director M. Knight Shyamalan's movie of the same name, people usually think that the sixth sense refers primarily to seeing ghosts.

In reality, few people see ghosts as full figures or living people. In ghost hunting, the sixth sense can include everything from the ability to hear ghosts whispering, to an internal visual image from the past, or even a "creepy feeling" that can't be explained.

Spirit

This word comes from the Latin, meaning "that which breathes," "that which animates life," or "the soul of the being."

Table Tapping, Table Tipping

A method of communicating with spirits, usually, several people sit around a table with their hands on it or hold hands on top of the table, and ask the spirits to communicate with them by tapping on the table, perhaps once for yes and twice for no. Others are successful in asking the ghosts to lift the table very slightly to show that they are present. The ghosts may tap their replies, move a Ouija-type platen, or use some other means to communicate with movement around the table.

Tarot

The history of the Tarot deck is still unclear. However, since its use in fourteenth century Italy, "Tarot" refers to playing cards that are also used for fortune-telling or divination.

Telekinesis

From a Greek word meaning any motion that is activated from a distance, this, technically, could describe a remote-controlled toy boat, so most people use the word psychokinesis for ghost research.

Vortex

Since the time of Descartes, this has indicated the rotation of cosmic energy around a central point or axis. Beginning in the mid-nineteenth century, the word "vortex" has meant any whirling movement of energy or particles. Some people use this term to explain lines or narrow cylinders that appear highlighted in ghost photos.

Bibliography

Books

Clark, Jerome. *Unexplained! 347 Strange Sightings, Incredible Occurrences, and Puzzling Physical Phenomena*. Detroit, Michigan: Visible Ink Press, 1993.

Hauck, Dennis William. *The National Directory of Haunted Places, Ghostly Abodes, Scary Sites, UFO landings, and Other Supernatural Locations*. New York, New York: Penguin Books, 1994.

Lankford, Andrea. *Haunted Hikes: Spine-Tingling Tales and Trails from North America's National Parks*. Santa Monica, California: Santa Monica Press, 2006.

Larios, Shellie. *Yellowstone Ghost Stories: Spooky Tales from the World's First National Park*. Helena, Montana: Riverbend Publishing, 2006.

Munn, Debra. *Ghosts on the Range: Eerie True Tales of Wyoming*. Helena, Montana: Pruett Publishing Company, 1989.

Whittlesey, Lee H. *Death in Yellowstone: Accidents and Foolhardiness in the First National Park*. Lanham, Maryland: Roberts Rinehart Publishers, 1995.

Web Resources

www.abovetopsecret.com

www.associatedcontent.com

www.bfro.net

www.books.google.com

www.buzzle.com

www.casperwyoming.info

www.crystalinks.com

www.deadwoodmagazine.com

www.dioceseofcheyenne.org

www.discovery.com

www.gabeltheatres.com

www.heartmountain.us

www.hschistory.org

www.jackalope.org

www.lakedesmet.com

www.legendsofamerica.com

www.lovetripper.com

www.meeteetsewy.com

www.nps.gov/DETO/index.html

www.omahaunt.com

www.outwestnewspaper.com

www.paganwiccan.about.com

www.paranormalstories.blogspot.com

www.redorbit.com

www.roadsideamerica.com

www.sacredsites.com

www.skullofskill.com

www.southpasscity.com

www.ssimf.com

www.sweetwaterlibraries.com

www.thecabinet.com

www.time.com

www.trailend.org

www.travelroads.com

www.ufo.cordmagic.com

www.washakiecounty.com

www.wendigoentertainment.com

www.worthotel.com

www.wyomingfrontierprison.org

www.wyomingtalesandtrails.com

www.wyomingterritorialpark.com

Index

EXIT
ONLY